She Ain't Heavy, She's My Mother

HARMONY BOOKS

NEW YORK

She Ain't Heavy, She's My Mother

A Memoir

Bryan Batt

Copyright © 2010 by Bryan Batt

Published in the United States by Harmony Books,
an imprint of the Crown Publishing Group,
a division of Random House, Inc., New York.
www.crownpublishing.com

HARMONY BOOKS is a registered trademark
and the Harmony Books colophon
is a trademark of Random House, Inc.

All photographs are from the Bryan Batt Collection,
except for page 223, top left: Joan Marcus ©
Disney Theatrical Productions.

Library of Congress Cataloging-in-Publication Data
Batt, Bryan.
She ain't heavy, she's my mother / Bryan Batt.—1st ed.
p. cm.
1. Batt, Bryan. 2. Actors—Louisiana—New Orleans—
Biography. 3. Gay actors—Louisiana—New Orleans—
Biography. I. Title.
PN2287.B387A3 2010
792.02'8092—dc22
[B]   2009049692
ISBN 978-0-307-58885-2

PRINTED IN THE UNITED STATES OF AMERICA

Design by Elizabeth Rendfleisch

1 3 5 7 9 10 8 6 4 2

First Edition

This book is dedicated to:
My mother, for her love;
Tom, for his love;
and New Orleans, the city I love!

Author's Note

I applied for and obtained my poetic license many years ago, and have remained in good standing ever since. It has served me well through my life so far, and I hope that, coupled with what some consider a healthy sense of humor, it will continue to do so. On occasion it's occurred to me that while life is happening around us or coming directly at us, we often are unable to take it all in, truly analyze it, and at the very same time live in the moment at hand. I've tried over and over again, but somehow my genetic makeup doesn't sustain such a process. I believe that is why we have memory, a mysteriously subjective system that allows us to recall the events that form our lives. Everyone's memory is different; each member of a family can experience the exact same event, and inevitably each individual will remember it slightly differently.

The following are my stories, and they are told as I remember them, or, rather, as I chose to remember and tell

Author's Note

them. They are based on factual events and actual people who helped bend and shape my life, but a couple of alterations here and there have been applied for the purpose of theatrical impact and to protect the innocent and the punishable. And, remember, I do have a license.

Contents

Prologue

MY FIRST MEMORY of my mother is of her cradling me as a baby and placing me ever so gently in my crib. I still can see the pale blue satin ribbon woven through the lace of her robe and the praying, bubble-headed, footy-pajama-wearing angels affixed to the wall of the nursery. Soft, calming tones flowed from her pink-painted mouth. Although I couldn't understand what she said, I was comforted and I remember deciding at that moment not to cry. I recall knowing that I was safe, that I was loved. Scientists and psychiatrists may question the validity of this brief yet crystal-clear remembrance, and under any normal circumstances they might have a point. But these circumstances are anything but normal. And they have never met my mother.

Most of my memories are fond ones, and for that I am grateful. Of course there have been tough and rough patches, but I choose not to dwell on those as they are a dissonant chord and I prefer harmony or at least a jazzy minor seventh. But those discordances are few; the good in my life thus far greatly outweighs the insignificant bad. Gayle Batt, the steel magnolia from whom I was fortunate to come forth into this world, made me the man I am today, and although I'm still discovering who and what that is, she gave me—or rather taught me by her example—some great life lessons: (1) defeat is not an option; (2) be happy in your own skin; (3) there is great beauty in great strength.

The bare facts are these: I was born on March 1, 1963, the second son to Gayle and John Batt of New Orleans, a handsome and stylish couple. I had what I then thought to be a typical middle-class to slightly upper-class upbringing until I realized that all kids didn't have a roller coaster in their backyard instead of a slide. My father's father founded Pontchartrain Beach in 1928, and for generations to come this amusement park was the biggest and best family entertainment in the Gulf South, that is, until Mickey entered the Everglades. I attended Isidore Newman School from kindergarten through twelfth grade, then, because of my father's failing health, stayed close to home and went to Tulane University. Then, fresh out of college, I moved to New York, completely green, with delusions of a career in the theatre. Blind ambition, combined with hard work and a great deal of sheer luck, enabled me to work for nearly twenty years on and off Broadway. When there was suddenly a significant lull in my stage career, I decided to follow another dream and temporarily moved back south with my partner, Tom Cianfichi (pronounced chee-on-fee-kee, which loosely translates to "have a fig"), to live part-time and open a fine gift/home furnishings shop called Hazelnut, named for my beloved maternal grandmother. From then on I was bicoastal, enjoying the vast dichotomy of the Big Apple and the Big Easy. I am a firm believer that life is an "and" proposition rather than an "or" proposition. However, while creating the shop during the excruciatingly hot, humid late summer and early fall of 2003, I would awaken in a cold sweat, questioning why I'd placed my portfolio as collateral on a business I knew nothing about. All I had was good taste, but thank heaven, Tom did know the business aspect, so those frantic panic attacks became fewer as the shop grew.

The real heart of the matter is this: we are capable of doing much more than most people expect of us. It's easy for people to place you in a category or a group and define you by that alone. I'm not sure whether this is typically American or simply human, but ever since one of my most memorable and life-changing conversations with my mother, I've tried at all costs to avoid being defined by other people's opinions or standards. Inadvertently, Mom taught me that, too.

My first day of kindergarten was an eye-opening entrée into a new world. When my mother questioned me about it, I asked her in all sincerity, "Why am I not colored, Jewish, and a girl?"

My unexpected and unfamiliar question literally cracked her perfectly applied ivory Alexander de Markoff foundation makeup, and tragically deflated the new coif in her black bouffant hair by at least an inch. In an effort to explain, she tilted her head in her signature style and said with a loving smile, "Honey, there are many different kinds of people in this great big wonderful world we live in—boys like you and girls like me; Christians like us; and Jewish people like . . . like . . . well, they are people who don't believe that Jesus is the son of God; white like us, and colored like . . . like . . . well, like Oralea; and we are all God's children. But the blue birds fly with the blue birds and the red birds with the red birds, and the yellow birds with the yellow birds and so on."

I was thoroughly confused by this analogy. "Hell, Mom, I'm not a bird!"

Now her makeup was really melting. "Language, doodle-bug," she managed to say through pursed frosted pink lips.

I kept trying to wrap my mind around how we were like birds and asked, "If God loves us all, and we are supposed to try to be like God, shouldn't we try to love everyone, or since we're talking birds, shouldn't we all fly together in the same big blue sky, no matter the color of our feathers or the size of our beaks?"

I got the characteristic Gayle Batt tilt, lilt, and smile in response. "You'll understand when you're older, peanut."

And although I tried, I never did.

And now I am an actor/designer/shop owner and live tricoastally in New Orleans, New York, and Los Angeles. I thank you for buying this book because it is an odd and expensive life to maintain.

In spring of 2006, Tom and I had planned a special trip to Paris as a token of our gratitude for selfless acts of heroism performed by my eldest godchild, Ramsey. I have seven godchildren—seven! When Katrina hit the city, we were on vacation in Sonoma and literally unable to return, so this young, highly competent nurse boarded up our shop and carriage house. Mom was panicking because her flight to Houston was canceled and Ramsey's car wouldn't start, so she took ours and drove Mom with her to Texas. By this point, Mom's need for another knee and hip replacement was apparent, and she could not sit for extended periods of time. Due to the record mass exodus, the pilgrimage that would normally take five to six hours was now doubled.

Needless to say, the forced exodus to Texas was no easy trip to the beach. Ramsey saved our store, our home, our car, and my mom—though not necessarily in that order. A trip to Paris was most definitely warranted.

With the trip just about a week away, I received a call from my agent in New York: "Hey, Bry, I have an audition for you for a pilot called *Mad Men*. The role is Salvatore Romano, the closeted art director at a fictional 1960s ad agency, Sterling Cooper, recurring possible series regular."

I asked when, and learned that the only days they were casting were in direct conflict with the Paris trip. This just reaffirms my belief that if you want an audition, the best thing to do is book a nonrefundable flight to a foreign country. Having mainly been a stage actor to this point, and sadly being able to count my television appearances on one hand, for the first time in my career I decided to choose life over show business. I told Bill that this trip to Paris was too important, but when I returned to the States, if the role had not been cast, I would love to audition, as I would be in New York to do a limited run off-Broadway. It was the first time I had chosen life over work in a very long time.

Prologue

As fate would have it, the creator, Matthew Weiner, and the director, Allen Taylor, had not found their "Sal," so weeks later, on lunch break from my show's rehearsals, I slicked my hair back, threw on a blazer with a jaunty pocket square, and headed downtown for the call. There was one audition, and the next day my agents called with the good news.

Two weeks later I was on set at Silver Cup Studios in Long Island City; the series itself would later be filmed in Los Angeles, surrounded by a picture-perfect office set circa 1960. The midcentury desks, the chairs, the art, all stunningly embodied the era. After finishing with hair and makeup, I changed into my period vintage suit and skinny tie, and was led to Don's office. Upon meeting Jon Hamm and shaking his hand, I thought, *Oh, they are doing this right*, and after the first take I was amazed at how spot-on he was in the role. Here was a perfectly prepared, extremely talented, highly skilled actor, and easy on the eyeballs to boot. I couldn't help thinking that if this series was picked up, this man would be a sensation, and deservedly so. Thrilled and nervous as hell, I hoped to be able to rise to the occasion and match the high standard he set, all the while trying to forget that my first job on Broadway was on roller skates, playing a singing and dancing boxcar in *Starlight Express*.

Show business makes no sense. Like love, it is fickle, divine, and heartbreaking. But when it clicks, when the stars align, it is incomprehensibly magical. All my life I've wanted to be an actor , an entertainer, and now, after years of work, and another year of praying and hoping that *Mad Men* would get the green light, I was driving through Hollywood to the L.A. Center Studios in my rented black Mini Cooper convertible, underneath the beautifully strange purple jacaranda trees. I actually slapped my own face to make sure I was not dreaming and that this was really my life unfolding before me. After a few days of working together, our cast started to bond like none other I've experienced. There suddenly grew a genuine sense of camaraderie which rarely if ever exists.

WE WERE IN the midst of filming episode four or five and I was in my trailer on the L.A. Center Studios set. Because I had not relocated or toured to another city besides New Orleans or New York for over fifteen years, I was having a difficult time adjusting to L.A., especially driving on the freeways. Before leaving New Orleans, I searched high and low through boxes and boxes of family photos at my mother's home for inspiration and comfort while away. Now I found myself looking at a 1960s photo of my mother eight months pregnant with me, martini and cigarette in her hands, just as women did in the early sixties and on our show. At a very early age I learned the story of how my mother badly wanted children but had trouble becoming pregnant. Temperatures were taken, and when the oven was right, Dad was called home from the office for "matinees," hot oil forced through fallopian tubes and the postcoital headstands. All this to bring forth my brother. Jay was referred to as the science baby, and due to the fact I was conceived at Seattle World's Fair in 1962, I was known as the love child.

Gazing at my reflection, seeing myself costumed circa 1960, I realized I looked just like my father. The face, the hair, the body—all John Batt. I have donned many a disguise for Mardi Gras, Halloween, and professionally on Broadway, but nothing compared to the strange mixture of emotions and memories that emerged when I saw myself as the physical double of my late father. I looked at my hands—they were his, the slight smile lines were beginning to form just as his, the gray temples framed my face identically. My entire physical being was a finely detailed replica, only I knew my heart was that of my mother. Just then my cell phone rang "When the Saints Go Marching In," which I had kept as my ring tone since Katrina. It was Mom.

"How's my Broadway and soon-to-be Hollywood TV star, doodlebug, I am so glad I caught you before you went on stage, or to practice, or whatever it is you do out there, but pet, don't forget to send something to Bailey and Kelly, your little nieces are so excited to be attendants to the Queen of the Spring Fiesta tonight. They looked so cute in their pantaloons, I almost started to cry. Just call Mr. Larry at the florist's and he'll know what to send to the girls . . . soft spring colors, of course, with no baby's breath . . . isn't it odd how some things just go out of fashion, things we loved, remember that Christmas tree we had on Pratt Drive in the seventies, we thought that baby's breath was so chic, and you know it was then, but now, no way, oh baby dear look at the time, I really must run coach, Mr. Albert has to do his magic on my hair for tonight, and I cannot be late, I declare that man is a miracle worker, a true artist. Call Mr. Larry, and honey, I am so proud of you . . . I love you."

And she was off; I almost could smell the Chanel perfume, which lingered well after her many flourished exits *con brio*.

"Love you too," I said.

There was a knock on the door, and it was Kyle, ever so respectfully letting me know that they were running late with filming and that there had been a freak accident on set. Part of the movable ceiling had fallen on our star Jon Hamm's head, and quite a few stitches were required, so the day's filming schedule would be revised shortly. Kyle told me to relax, as I would not be called to set for quite some time; in fact, my scene might be rescheduled for another day entirely. As fate would have it, Jon is a killer trouper and returned that day to continue filming. As instructed, I placed the floral order for my nieces and thought of my introduction to the New Orleans tradition of the Spring Fiesta, often referred to as A Night in Old New Orleans.

Reclining, my intent was to take a short nap because the evening before had been a *Mad Men* get-together, and as can happen it ended with me being over-served. But I couldn't rest because my mind was swirling with memories and residual hooch. Maybe seeing my father's face in the mirror combined with my mom's doting call made it impossible to sleep. Memory is a strange friend, either the kind you sometimes wish would not call when they do, or the sort you dream could stay and play forever. Luckily I had my computer and some time to play with "the misty water-colored memories in the corners of my mind."

The Spring Fiesta
or Rites of Passage

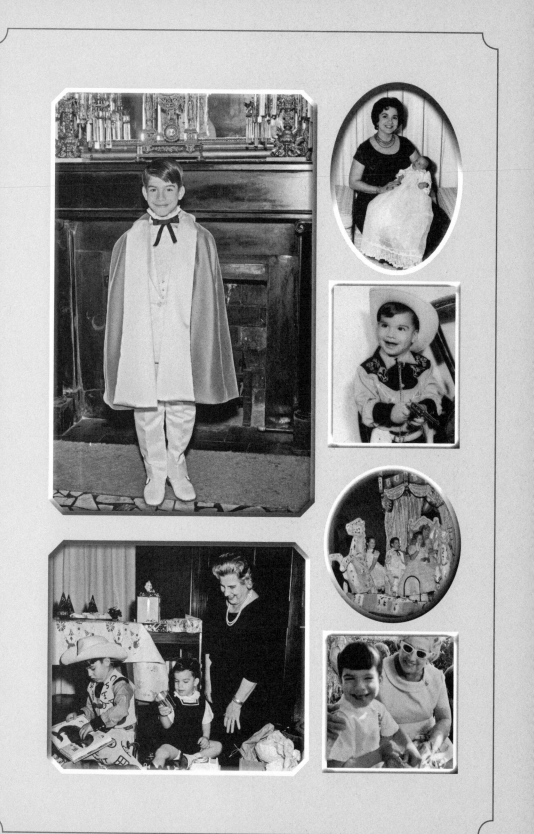

THE RITE OF PASSAGE for most Southern boys entails hunting and killing a deer or a duck or another random woodland creature. Mine involved pink satin, a glittering papier-mâché float, and a dozen young girls in hoop skirts. I didn't think it was odd.

After picking me up from school, my mom would often stop by my aunt Vilma's house on Fontainebleau Drive for refreshments and a visit. This was her old family home-stead, a modest but impeccably kept three-story columned structure nestled among a few glorious live oaks, dripping with Spanish moss. Now it was under the management of her elder sister, Vilma, and Vilma's husband, Stock-ton, aka Uncle Bru, a warm, kind gentleman and a proud Virginia-born descendent of Thomas Jefferson. His accent occasionally reminded me of the cartoon rooster Foghorn Leghorn. I'd often hear, "Brannnnnn, ha aw ya sun I say good ta seeya." The dwelling was graced by their three beautiful redheaded daughters, each completely different from the other two, and each the object of my wild childish crush.

I always had Chek Cola or Barq's root beer, served in a freezing aluminum mug, and my mother always had steaming hot black coffee, even with the temperature sweltering in the upper nineties, and the air syrupy with humidity. But one day in early September would prove to be special. One of my favorite cousins, Alyce Leigh Jefferson, was in town from college.

For generations in our family, it has been the custom to substitute the letter *y* for *i* in first names. Gail was Gayle, Alice was Alyce, and Brian was Bryan. Nobody could recall when this practice started, or why we did it, but no one dared buck the system, no matter how impossible it made it to purchase manufactured personalized bicycle license plates, pencils, or stickers at the TG&Y dime store.

LeeLee, as Alyce Leigh was affectionately called, was the typical good girl, and with her parents' encouragement she decided to take a semester's leave from Spring Hill University to return home and make her debut. Nobody questioned this arrangement. Many young Southern ladies of a certain ilk actually believe college credit should be given to those who dutifully and with great aplomb embrace the archaic practice of the "coming out."

The age of the *juenes filles* bow to society is customarily during the junior year of college; any older and the peaches are often bruised. Certain customs vary by region, as does the length of the debut season. The longest is in New Orleans. It spans from August clear through to the stroke of midnight on Shrove Tuesday, months and dates changing annually due to the irresponsible placement of Ash Wednesday, Lent, and Easter. This tradition is so firmly entrenched that for those families whose fortunes have been squandered or lost over generations, inconceivable sacrifices are made to continue or, in newer families, initiate the proper debut. In some instances mortgages, both second and third, have been sought, children denied college educations, and family heirlooms sold at auction at a fraction of their monetary—not to mention their sentimental—value, to afford the rite. Wherever, however, and whoever, at some point the girls are gussied up and primped into white gowns, then paraded with great pomp, thus signifying their position, virtue, and availability for matrimony. Most of these privileged young ladies curtsy graciously, grow up, have careers, raise families, and move on with their lives, although some are doomed to glance constantly back throughout their lives, desperately seeking to recapture the glimmer of a tinseled fleeting moment.

The current season was mounting into full swing; the big extravagant soirées at the country club would soon follow, not to mention the lavish Mardi Gras *bals masques*. And, although she would be invited to many of these functions, LeeLee would have a simple, elegant ladies' afternoon tea at home, hosted by her mother and grandmother, whom we all affectionately called Moozie. Vilma saw to it that her daughters had what she never did nor could have, whether they desired it or not. So the sprays of yellow roses matched the pale yellow silk of LeeLee's hand-sewn gown, and when she was to be queen of a carnival ball, she would most definitely have the pristine white canopy from front door to curbside, even if Vilma had to sew it herself on the Singer. I always admired her graceful determination of will. Like mother, like daughter, like daughter.

Moments after Mom and I breezed into Aunt Vilma's parlor, a bright red Volkswagen bug barreled into the driveway, the horn tooting a high-pitched "shave and a haircut, two bits." A few seconds later the kitchen screen door was flung open by my miniskirted cousins, Paula and Debbie. Paula, with a wickedly bawdy sense of humor and an infectious laugh, was my favorite babysitter. Her older sister, Debbie, was Twiggy-thin, high-strung, and artsy.

Not a minute later, as if on cue, the front door opened and in sashayed Moozie, a zaftig but handsome woman with the silverest of silver hair intensely teased to create the perfect asymmetrical swoop, framing her heavily powdered face. Affixed on the bridge of her delicate nose— about her only physical attribute that could be described as delicate with the exception of her ankles—were glittering, rhinestone-encrusted, cat-eyed bifocals that she wore religiously until the day she died, thirty years later. Frantic kisses, bear hugs, cheek pinching, long legs, flaming red hair, and waves of Shalimar perfume filled the room as the iced tea, hot chicory coffee, and soft drinks were poured. We all gathered around the kitchen table as if assembling for some monumental news.

Vilma, tapping her spoon aside a cut pressed glass, called the meeting to order. Mother sat up straight at attention and gave us the tilt, "Yes, Madam Chairman," to a burst of giggles, which prompted Moozie to exclaim, "Now come on, y'all are just playing ladies."

This was Moozie's usual response whenever anyone was goofing off or being silly, practices for which she had little or no patience. Moozie was a strong but loving woman who, at a very early age, worked to support her family during the Depression and on through the Eisenhower years, in a time and place where "ladies" didn't labor. Singlehandedly she became the foremost dance maven of the Big Easy, at one time practically teaching all of the city's children in one of her several successful studios. The iron-clad rules and regulations that she initiated for her schools reflected those she instituted for her family as well as her life. In keeping with her German heritage, they were to be followed and never bent or broken. She never really had the luxury to play, "ladies" or otherwise. I always adored the fact that the German translation of my beloved grandmother Moozie's name, Hazel Nuss, is "hazel nut," and adored my great-grandparents even more for having the rare sense of humor to name her just that.

The room finally settled down long enough for Vilma to announce that her daughter, Alyce Leigh Jefferson, had been asked to reign as Queen of the Spring Fiesta the coming season, and although not a Mardi Gras social club, it was one in which some very "fine" families still participated.

Annually, on a sultry spring evening, New Orleanian ladies and their daughters of age would, and still do, don antebellum costumes and, with their Ashley Wilkes–attired escorts, parade through the gaslit, decaying, narrow streets of the decadent French Quarter, fruitlessly attempting to revel in the traditions of the Old South. Girls on papier-mâché floats wearing hoop skirts trimmed with polyester synthetic blended fabric, lace and bows, would wave and toss daisies and gladiola stalks to the oblivious, inebriated tourists, the stoned, love-beaded hippies, and the sequin-pastied strippers of Bourbon Street. An odd combination of procession and audience at best. However, beneath the radiant sparkling of a flower-festooned rhinestone diadem, the view can be so much altered. Oh yes, the grand splendor of our long-lost Dixie was recaptured.

In addition to LeeLee's invitation, her sisters were asked to wear sherbet-hued gowns and be *des demoiselles* (ladies in waiting) in the court. But there was more. The monumental, life-altering information was yet to be dispensed. A hush fell over the bustling kitchen for a second time, as all the lightly mascaraed eyes in the room softly shifted and set their gaze upon me. Ceremoniously my mother rose, and I slumped as she announced, with a lump in her throat and a tear in her eye, "Dahlin, now it is my pleasure to announce that you, my sweet gallant son, young Bryan Mackenroth Batt, have been invited to have the honor of being the first-ever male page to the Queen of the Spring Fiestaaaaa!" Her voice rose to an effervescent cry of elation. Hugs from all the fair family femmes followed, as if I had just been inducted into an ancient, mysterious secret sorority. And I most definitely had, for as soon as the proclamation had been made I was instantaneously, and with gravest solemnity, sworn to absolute secrecy. Such information was considered top secret, hush-hush. The slightest slip of the tongue could render these illustrious invitations rescinded, annulling the social coup for which my aunt and mother had covertly campaigned, of having four family members in one court. Nevertheless, it was a court and a coup, and I accepted with pride.

At school, I skipped through the checkerboard linoleum corridors with an impish grin that declared, *I've got a secret, and I'll simply burst if I don't tell someone.*

The pressure of attempting to contain such vital and valuable data filled me with a fresh feeling of importance and belonging, but as the months gradually crept toward the blessed event, the desire to share my extraordinary information grew from a smoldering simmer into a raging, bubbling boil. But I kept my ever-flapping tongue from uttering a single syllable of my secret through Halloween, Christmas, and Mardi Gras.

The single incident that propelled me over the edge took place at the home of Miss Inez, my grandmother's confidante and seamstress for decades. The very moment I gazed upon the sketch of my glorious costume, a mid-nineteenth-century azure satin evening suit with a cutaway coat, a rhinestone-buttoned vest, a frilly white ruffled lace jabot, and a jaunty, deep velvet ankle-length cape, I was a goner. Mr. René, who was an old family friend and had designed numerous costumes and evening gowns for the ladies in our family for years, had created this vision for me. This was my first introduction to the fabulous world of art, fashion, and theatrical pageantry.

As we sat in Miss Inez's modestly decorated living room, cluttered with plastic statues of every Catholic saint imaginable, from the blissfully ecclesiastical to the absolutely tortured, the only audible sounds were the breathy whispered *oohs* and *ahhs* that accompanied the antici-pated revealing, until Moozie broke through the wordless smolder.

"I hate to tell y'all this, but that Mediterranean blue will just not show up under the dim gaslights of the French Quarter, no, it simply will not. We don't want him to get lost against the night sky, not our boy, and since LeeLee will be wearing white, naturally, as will the two little girl attendants, I think Bryanny boy should wear the palest of blush pink satin. Yes, yes, yes. That will match the pink papier-mâché roses on the Queen's float, and the little girls' pink sashes. We really should phone Mrs. Fitzmor-ris and Mrs. de La Verne and get samples of the fabric so it all coordinates, there's nothing I hate more than pastel color clash. Oh, and instead of daises they could toss baby pink carnations, they're not that much dearer, and there is nothing I hate more than the stench of old daisy water."

I don't recall any form of protestation. Why shouldn't a six-year-old boy be dressed as a powdered pink pim-pernel? Moozie's vast knowledge of costumes and color palette was indisputable, as was her will. Therefore, Miss Inez mumbled her accord through a pin-filled mouth, and Mother, not one to dissent frequently from her mother's judgment or the grave lapse thereof, graced us with her signature tilt and smile of concurrence.

Now there was no stopping me. I just had to tell some-one about the parade and my costuming. I had to tell Leann.

One of my most lasting childhood friends is Leann Opotowsky, a sharp-witted girl whose last name was forever unpronounceable by my parents. Aesthetically, we could have been siblings. She unfortunately shared my wide-mouthed cartoonish countenance. Luckily time and providence allowed us to evolve into more attractive young adults, with the obvious omission of puberty.

Resolved to impart my most cherished confidence, I concluded the ideal moment would naturally be recess, as opposed to the silence of nap time or the furor of art class, in which I'd been painting crude yet colorful primitives of crowns, flowers, and hoop skirts for months. In retrospect, had Miss Fife, my teacher, been more of a climbing daughter of the Confederacy, she might have detected the glaringly apparent signals. Nevertheless, during cookies and milk I whispered to Leann that I had to tell her a GREAT BIG SECRET and to meet me at the beginning of recess at the top of the monkey bars. Because we were the most fearless scramblers in class, we could be assured of privacy. Secrets and the ability to both keep and share them are of great importance in kindergarten, as I was soon to find out. The hand bell rang out, recess was declared, and we raced to the jungle gym and began our ascent from opposing sides so that we would meet at the very apex, leaving the other children behind and below. There was precious little time for me to spill, so breathlessly I rattled off as rapidly as possible every last detail of the illustrious anticipated festivities, my majestic involvement, and the imperative call for confidentiality. It's a strange lesson to learn so young, but one man's fortune is sometimes another's fertilizer. Leann's wide-eyed, incredulous stare met mine as she shuddered.

"That's *it*? That's your big secret? You're going to wear a tooty-fruity costume and give flowers to complete strangers, and *that* is supposed to be fun? Whoop-de-do! I'd rather clean erasers."

Stunned and shattered, I could only muster a paltry retort. "Oh yeah . . . well, I get to miss a whole day of school."

"That," she replied, "could be rather groovy."

"No duh, but you can't tell anyone. I mean it. Not Miss Fife. Not even your mom."

She promised, but said that she found the entire affair "rather silly" and "rather unimportant."

At quite a significantly early age, Leann had modeled her persona after Kay Thompson's "Eloise." She had a little pug dog like Eloise, and a turtle like Eloise, and frequently overused the word "rather," just like the mischievous, bobby-socked heroine of the Plaza Hotel.

Descending the monkey bars, I felt slightly relieved to have finally told someone, but dismayed by her reaction, disappointed that she hadn't found my news "rather fantastic and rather extraordinary, don't you know." However, Leann always spoke her mind and always kept her promise.

Finally the anticipated day, April 23, arrived, and by the time I woke up, Jay was already on the bus to school, Dad had dashed off to work, and Mom was in the painstaking process of "putting on her face," while Oralea, now cooking breakfast, had come to help with the frantic preparations and organization of the day. She was a diminutive, speedy, and dynamic cocoa-complexioned lady with a smartly cropped Afro slightly graying at the temples. The early symptoms of osteoporosis had given her a slight hump and a bowing of the head, so that her dancing eyes always appeared to be looking upward, focused to the heavens. She was the most requested caterer at the finest catering company in New Orleans, and she met my parents while arranging the trays of hors d'oeuvres for their engagement party. They took an instant liking to each other, and had gotten along beautifully ever since. No party or special day was complete without Oralea, and when, in years to come, we moved into a big new home of my father's design, she decided to work for our family full-time. Although my mother was the "lady of the house," it was Oralea who singlehandedly ran the entire show. I idolized her amazing coiffeuring skills. Throughout the week, her hair would change in length, cut, and color. I didn't know then that they were wigs; I just thought she was incredible.

She made the best sunny side up eggs, coddled in a pan of butter, alongside creamy cheese grits slathered with even more butter, and thickly sliced salty Virginia fried ham. While I lapped it up, she reminded me of my manners, telling me to slow down, this home isn't a barn, to use my fork and knife, that they weren't put there just for decoration, and then coyly declared, "So, little mister, tonight's parade's the big affair, you're going to get all done up and ride that big ol' float with your Nan-Nan's girl LeeLee. Honey child, every eye in the whole French Quarter is going to be fixed on you."

It suddenly occurred to me that while a minuscule part

of me was a tad apprehensive of the approaching parade, the vast majority of my small soul was consumed with the idea of being the focus of hundreds, possibly thousands, of adoring eyes. With a small dollop of cheese grits dripping from my chin and with a big inhale of the fresh balmy morning air, I sighed deeply and said, "Oralea, I just can't wait, this is the most important day of my life."

She suddenly burst into peals of hearty laughter, with a cackle that would have silenced a hen house.

"Ooh baby, I declare, what mess have they got you thinking?"

She stopped for a moment, then smiled just long enough to show a glimpse of her big teeth, nestled down next to me in the breakfast room banquette, gently placed her forehead to mine, and whispered, "Listen to Miss Oralea, you live your life right, and almost every day can be the most important day of your life, you hear me, and you can take that advice downtown on the streetcar and deposit it at the Whitney Bank, for true."

She always had sage life advice that frequently blew right through my ears, but I loved some of her sayings. If someone wasn't too bright, she'd say, "That child is dumber than a bucket of hair." If someone would try to pull a fast one on her, she'd say, "Don't sneeze on my cupcake and tell me it's frosting." Or if something struck her as odd or bizarre, she'd say, "'Tain't natural, it's like a chicken dating a dog." Sometimes, though, I just didn't get it. For instance, if she felt tired, she'd say, "Put tired on top of tired, and get your dancin' shoes on."

"Now let's get cookin' with gas, Little Lord Fauntleroy,

eat them eggs 'cause we got to get you all hosed down and dressed, then your mama's taking you with her to the Hair-etage Beauty Salon to get all slicked up for tonight, and take those elbows off the table . . . Now where did your mama put them little pink roses for her hair?"

With a flash, the room was filled with an asphyxiating blast of Lanvin's signature fragrance, Arpege, as my frilly-robed mother swirled in. Restraint was not her forte, especially in the use of perfume; more was more, as was also true of my father with Dior's Eau Savage cologne. It must have been the last remnant of French ancestry in their blood. In the car, the excess of aroma could prove lethal; we had to have my brother's window rolled down, his round face to the wind like a pup, despite the raging heat or the gas-guzzling Cadillac air-conditioning system, in order to prevent an asthma attack.

She had clearly interrupted her makeup ritual, because I could literally see only one eye and one brow painted on the blank canvas of her bisque-toned base. In one of her manicured hands she held a switch of black hair that matched her own color perfectly, and in the other a pair of white-ruffled pantaloons.

"Lea!" the one-eyed woman exclaimed. "Where did we put the hoop skirt? I thought it was under the bed, but now it's nowhere to be found, Bryan needs a bath, I look like a Cyclops, and our appointment with Philippe is in less than a half an hour, please Jesus don't let it rain tonight."

Panic had obviously set in.

"Now don't get your liver in a quiver, keep your bees in your basket, and the dogs won't bite."

"What?"

"Keep your girdle on, missy. Go and finish up your pretty little face, I'll bathe the boy and find that hoop before you can eat a biscuit, and as for Philippe, let prissy-man wait. It ain't like he got any more important hair to do all up today but yours."

"Dawlin, you're an angel on earth, I Sewanee you are." She blew kisses and whisked herself away.

After my quick rinse, as Oralea went out back to the carport to sleuth the missing hoop, and while Mother was affixing eyelashes, a procedure that demanded the utmost concentration, I slyly retrieved the hoop skirt from underneath my bed. It's strange, I had absolutely no inhibitions or insecurities about playing with the contraption, or wearing it, whether as a skirt or a giant mushroom-like costume. It was a fascinatingly fun new thing that, although linked to the wonderful world of historic feminine lingerie, could be so much more. But in the end, I unquestionably knew better than to enter my parents' quarters and amuse myself with their personal effects without permission, so I stealthily returned it to its proper place.

From the beginning, my parents made it clear that I could always confide in them. They were my parents and they loved me, no matter what. They were repeatedly tried and tested by both sons, and for the most part, they remained true to their promise. But in this case I remained silent. Later, when it was discovered in its proper dwelling back under my parents' bed, no one bothered to wonder at this miracle amid the scurry and confusion.

Like the winds of Hurricane Betsy, we were soon racing southward to the famed beauty salon and antique boutique called Hair-etage, owned by Mr. Philippe. While the ladies waited for their cherished appointments, they could browse and purchase old Staffordshire porcelain figurines, silver Corinthian-column candlesticks, Louis XV crystal chandeliers, or, when seated under the stream-lined, state-of-the-art hair dryers, they could experience the comfort of a newly upholstered and puffed-up bergère or a Queen Anne wingbacked chair. The only drawback to this mecca of beauty and art was the presence of a precocious boy dragged by his mother to witness and partake in an afternoon of hair-washing, combing, setting, teasing, and shellacking.

"Now, doodlebug, when we arrive, please put on your best manners and behave like a good little gentleman, sit next to me and don't run around the salon like a wild Indian. Mr. Philippe's store is filled to the gills with very expensive things that we don't want to break and have to buy and make Daddy very angry, do we?"

"I promise to be good. Can we go to the Camellia Grill on the way home?"

"If you wait patiently while I get my hair done, and sit still while Mr. Philippe cuts and styles yours, we will go to the Grill for hamburgers and chocolate freezes."

She should have known that even the tempting bribe of Camellia's was not sufficient to ensure my complete co-operation; nothing on earth could be incentive enough to constrain my bull-in-the-china-shop reputation. These were the days prior to the mass dispensing of Ritalin. I know for a fact that as an infant, tiny shots of bourbon were mixed into my bedtime bottle, so I would not have blamed my parents if they had attempted to further medicate me. In retrospect, I was a super ball of energy, a Tasmanian devil on speed, and my boundless antics often elicited my mother's highest curse: "Judas priest, son, can you sit still for a cotton-pickin' minute, is that at all possible? I Sewanee, you and your brother are driving me to distraction!"

Sometimes I thought that it might have helped release some of her mounting frustration and stress if she could just cry out the occasional *fuck, shit,* or *piss,* which I had mastered so effortlessly. Now I know that vulgar language is a nasty addiction for anyone, especially a preschooler, but I'm not completely to blame. Since my birth, I had repeatedly overheard alarmingly florid vocalization flowing from my father after his third J&B scotch on the rocks. He was a handsome, thunderous, imposing, manly man. Sentimental, he drank J&B scotch in honor of his two sons, Jay and Bryan, and by the ripe age of three, I had mastered gutter vocabulary. I didn't understand the meaning of these words, but I fully grasped their dramatic impact on others, especially my big brother. He would frequently wrestle me beneath his husky frame and tickle me mercilessly until I'd expel a litany of expletives.

"Shit, fuck, piss . . . shit, fuck, piss . . . damn it to hell . . . biiiiiitch!!!"

When this would happen, Mother would explain that even though Daddy sometimes spoke like that, it was not proper language for a polite young boy.

When she was a little girl, she never heard language

like that. Her father, who had unfortunately gone to his reward long before I was born, on no account ever raised his voice, much less cussed. Never. Ever. Ever. "You must do as I say, doodlebug, and not as he does. Learn to control your mind, your tongue, and various other parts of your anatomy, and you'll grow up to be a fine young gentleman, like your papa," she reminded me. Those conversations never did much to curb my cussing, and I still think the occasional expletive would have done my mother good. But it's possible her rosebud of a mouth was simply not capable of forming, much less verbalizing, the necessary sequence of consonants and vowels. Besides, if she did use such language, there probably wouldn't be enough concealer to hide the cracks.

SOON OUR BEIGE station wagon screeched into the manicured parking area of the Hair-etage's sky-blue Victorian cottage. The scent of Confederate jasmine that enveloped every balustrade of the filigreed wrought-iron entrance stairway, coupled with the potted gardenia topiaries, topped by my mother's overpowering perfume, made the air dizzying, and I was forced to hold her hand not just for parental assurance, but for sheer physical support.

Upon entry, Mother was escorted away by salon minions to be shampooed, conditioned, and rinsed while I was fawned over, patted on the head, and seated in an armchair that was obviously a reproduction, along with many *Highlights, Vogue,* and *Modern Salon* magazines. All of these were entertaining, but soon I felt the instinctual desire to explore, and later was discovered with perm rods up my nose, imitating the walruses we had recently witnessed in the Audubon Zoo. Unlike the respective floral and spice smells of my mother and father's toiletries, I preferred the strident chemical smells of perm solution, turpentine, or, better yet, the pungent and exotic aroma of gasoline. When confronted with a look that seemed to say, *Silly monkey, what are you into now?* I had no response but to pull the perm rods out of my nostrils and stammer, "Mom, you look beautiful." To which the room of ladies collectively released an adoring sigh, all except the shampoo wench, Miss Amber, who had just about had it with my antics all afternoon. Mom did look stunning, though, even if she was my mom. Her raven hair was piled high, the swirls punctuated with baby pink sweetheart roses, and cascading down the left side of her neck was a cluster of sausage curls. It was the perfect marriage of antebellum and Vidal Sassoon. As she was seated to have her makeup retouched for the evening, Mr. Philippe swaggered in and made a musky appearance in the doorway. He was the model on which Warren Beatty must have based his character for *Shampoo*. He stood six foot two, with longish shaggy brown tresses, piercing blue eyes, tight, bell-bottomed, lace-up-crotched suede jeans, and open-shirted hairy chest. He was the antithesis of every woman's husband in the room. They all secretly lusted for him. He knew it, and worked it. After circling around me at least three or four times, messing and tossing my bangs, his deep voice rasped, "So this is Mr. Bryan. How are you, little man? Fab hair." He stopped dead in his tracks and started to shake his mane. "Oh, Gayle baby, I can't do it, please don't make me, I can't cut it, you've just got to let it grow, grow, grow. If he were mine, this thick hair would graze his shoulder at the least." He bent down and fixed me with a knowing stare. "You'd dig that, little man, wouldn't you?"

Before I could utter a single syllable of agreement, Mom chimed in, "Oh . . . uh . . . Philippe, baby, if it were up to me, I'd say . . . of course . . . far out . . . let it all hang . . . out."

Who was this flower-adorned impostor pretending to be my mother? She babbled on, "Philippe . . . baby . . . you know me . . . I'm . . . hip . . . hep . . . cool, but Johnny would never allow it. He's kind of . . . you know . . . square." Her index fingers tracing the shape in midair, she continued. "He likes his boys to look like boys, and no confusion. Dig? So please, honey . . . baby, for me, give him a boy's regular number three, and slick it to the side. And Bryan, please sit still."

He complied reluctantly, trimming, cutting, and edging so that my white-walled ears as well as my previously hidden eyes would be completely visible, finishing off the process with pomade and All-Set spray against his will and better judgment. He was a firm believer that the wet head was dead, long live the dry look, but not in this case. Looking in the mirror, I saw my shiny black hair severely parted on the side and plastered down, set and sprayed into a Baby Hitler look. Why couldn't I have cool hair and long sideburns like Mr. Philippe? But suddenly we were out of the salon, in the station wagon, and racing to the river's bend. Over the years Mom would have many different hairdressers; it was the one relationship that she had serious trouble with, all her life.

The Camellia Grill is the last of the countertop service diners in the Big Easy. Its daily specials, like slow-cooked red beans and rice with sausage or pork chops (traditionally served only on Mondays), are enjoyed by multitudes of locals and Tulane students, as are the fluffiest of omelettes whipped to soufflé perfection in blenders, the Camellia's perfect hamburgers, and my favorite: icy chocolate freezes. But the main attraction is the white-coated waiters and their grand presentation of drinking straws. With magician-like agility, half of the protective paper wrapping is sheathed away, and the red striped end is presented with a ceremonious flourish to the enraptured customer.

While devouring what would have to suffice for supper, but not as elegantly and as "pinkies up" as Mother dined, I kept asking her why she suddenly changed the way she spoke and acted when Mr. Philippe winced at the thought of cutting my hair.

"Dawlin'," she said, "it's not really white lies at all, no sirree, it's like playacting, sometimes you have to pretend a little and tell people what they want to hear in order to get what you need or want. I know that must sound crazy, but it's true, and it works. If it doesn't, it sometimes helps to play dumb. Just look at how handsome you look with that perfect young gentleman's haircut that both your daddy and I adore, if I didn't quickly say something in a way that Mr. Philippe would appreciate, we might still be at his shop fretting over every last hair on your precious little coconut head and not enjoying these tasty treats."

That said, she picked up the crispiest French fry and bit it, smiled, and winked. Her unconventional methods strangely made sense, and in the future I, too, would sometimes call on these wiles to escape and avoid a sticky or possibly confrontational situation. Neither of us seemed to notice or pay any mind to the occasional stares we received from the other diners at the counter. After all, doesn't every gluey-haired boy have a late-afternoon snack with his overly perfumed, coiffed, and florally adorned mother before dressing in attire one hundred years out of fashion?

"Jiminy Christmas, lamb chop, look at the time, we've got to skedaddle on home or we'll never ever ever be ready in time! Dear Jesus, Mary, and Joseph, I realize you've got other situations to contend with, like the war in Vietnam, but please don't let it rain tonight, not just for me and Bryanny-boy, but for LeeLee and all the other girls whose special night this is, thank you, amen!"

As soon as she paid the lethargic keeper of the antique cash register and tipped Claude, our regular and masterful waiter, the glass-paneled doors swung open and we were off again, homeward bound at last. Speeding along Carrollton Avenue, Mother repeatedly asked me, as she would do for the rest of my days in the Crescent City, what I thought to be the most efficient route home, the highway or straight onward or the short cut. No matter what my response was, she would inevitably do the very opposite. She didn't do this just with me or with directions; she'd ask almost anyone's ideas on any subject, it didn't matter who it was, a relative, a friend, or a stranger, receive their honest opinion, then take a completely different course of action. I guess she wanted to hear all possible options, make people feel that their views and thoughts truly mattered, then do exactly what she had planned from the get-go. Nevertheless we proceeded straight forth along Bayou St. John and City Park with the faint beginnings of a pink and mandarin sunset ahead.

Our heavy oak front door opened to the tinkling sound of scotch, ice, and leaded crystal as Dad greeted us in his tuxedo. Obviously he had finished the daily afternoon checkers game ritual with my brother, from which, for reasons of immaturity and inexperience, I was often excluded. Dad bowed at the waist with a waving courtier's gesture from his left hand, while his right clutched the tumbler holding the last sip of cocktail.

"Welcome home, my royal family, what the hell took you so long?"

Mom fluttered hurriedly past him with a flash of a kiss, making a breathless comment about "watching the language in front of the B-O-Y." She trotted down the corridor, glancing over her shoulder, giving her best tilt and lilt.

"Boo, there's no time to waste; I can get myself dressed, if Oralea pressed my pantaloons, and all you need to do is zip me, but in the meantime get Bryanny in his costume, it's hanging in the hall closet, and please, pretty please, pour me a tall stiff one."

Dad made some remark about how he had a "stiff one" for her, and after a few moments of explanation, Mother finally understood the low-brow jest, sighed, rolled her overly painted eyes with disapproval, and disappeared into their bedroom. Although my father was not an active participant in the daily aspects of parenting, when his help was desperately needed, he always stepped up to the plate.

I had just gotten undressed when I heard the loud, pseudo-operatic bellow of my father. He had obviously located my ensemble.

"Jesus Christ, Gayle, did you fall out of a tree and hit your head? Have you lost your ever-loving mind? Pink? For crying out loud, what kind of boy—"

"Honey, hush, there's no time to argue, I tried like the dickens to get her to change her mind, but this is the color that Miss Le Blanc insisted on. Anyway it's done, you know you can't argue with the captain of a parade, much less that biddy. Now be a doll and fix me that cocktail, and dress Bryan, and what about Jay-bird? Is he dressed and ready?"

She was on a mission of diversion, and in a race with her unyielding nemesis, the clock. She was in fifth gear and rapidly firing off her commands.

Carrying a fresh scotch, Dad entered my small room with my costume in tow. Resigned, he surprisingly had little difficulty finessing the abundant snaps and hooks, each punctuated by a slight grunt and exhale of eighty-proof. I was soon complete, ankle-length rose-tinted velvet cape and all. The absurdity of my costume must have worn off, since Dad grinned and said, "Son, we are almost done. Hey, I'm a poet and I didn't know it, but my feet show it, they're such long fellows."

He chuckled, and although the joke was lost on me, I was eager for the opportunity to share a rare laugh with my father. Then he summoned my big brother.

"Jay-boy, how's that tie coming, come on in here, son, and show Pops how you're doing." Jay lumbered into the room, struggling with a hideous polyester maroon necktie that he had fashioned into what looked more like a hangman's noose than a Windsor knot. Upon seeing me in full regalia, he gasped and laughed with such intensity that for a moment we feared the start of an asthma attack.

"Oh . . . my . . . God . . . that is the most pansy-looking outfit I've ever seen!"

Dad was in no mood to be reminded of how Liberace I looked. He sipped and grunted, "Son, go check on your mother."

"But, Pops, it's pink, it's sissy pink, and what kind of boy wears that kind of lacy stuff around his neck?"

Having a notoriously explosive temper, Dad was now biting down on the back of his teeth, causing his jaw to jut forward in an instinctive reaction of absolute rage, traceable to other species of higher primates.

"Godammit! Obviously your little brother does! Listen, son, if you know what's good for you, you'll shut up, go check on your mother, fill this glass to the top with J&B with three ice cubes, no more, no less, and fix that sorry-ass excuse for a tie. *Now!*"

Jay bolted from the room, tumbler in hand.

For a few moments there was just silence while Dad just stared at me. He bent down and placed his strong hands, like two huge bunches of bananas, on each of my frail shoulders, raised his head so that we were eye-to-eye, but no words were spoken, just a slight shake of the head, scotch-scented breath, and an expression of confused defeat. Then he asked for a hug. After which he rose to his full height, looked down at his silly son, once again sighing and slightly shaking his head, but no words.

Jay, panting breathlessly, reentered my small yellow room with a brimming cocktail in hand as a peace offering, and as Dad fixed his tie, he eagerly added, "Pops, if you think Bryan looks stupid, wait until you get a load of Mom, her skirt can't even fit through the door, how's she gonna fit in the car?"

"Trust me, son, knowing your mother, she'll manage just fine. All right, boys, you know what the shepherd said?" That was our cue, so together we all chimed, "Let's get the flock out of here!"

Just then we heard the hysterical cry of my frantic and tardy antebellum-dressed mother, her usual lilting Southern accent now magnified by scotch whiskey and ancestral garb. We piled into Dad's sporty forest-green El Dorado, Mom's skirt taking up most of the backseat, leaving me just enough room so my cape wouldn't get mooshed. Jay had to sit in front, and, owing to the high level of perfume, was allowed to roll the window down just enough so his nose could get fresh air, but so that the gusts of wind would not muss up Mom's hairdo. On the trip down to the French Quarter, my parents discussed possible traffic-avoiding routes while they sipped from their "go cups." Lead-footed Dad told Mom over and over how beautiful she looked, and like a teenager she flirted back, a pleasant change from the increasing bickering. The tide turned a little when he asked the cost of the new black velvet gown, but she appeased him by adding that she had reused and beaded the lace from her wedding gown as the trim, and the faux-silk clusters of pink roses were from the Oriental Trading Company, and cost less than a song.

When Mom and I got out of the car, we were whisked away by a similarly dressed older woman. Before she joined her sister and comrades on their float titled "Mammy's Little Baby," Mom pulled out her pink lipstick from her dainty petit-point handbag, and, as she painted my naturally red lips pink, instructed me always to wear my white gloves while on the float, always to follow the Queen, cousin LeeLee, and help her with her long train, and, most importantly, to smile, smile, smile. Then she produced a flowery embroidered hanky for me to blot with, and she was off.

Before I knew it, I was in a room filled with young ladies all dressed in hoop skirts trimmed in lace and flowers with matching frilly parasols in every pastel color imaginable. The scene resembled an explosion in a Deep South sherbet factory. Nothing was dark or severe. Light sky-blue and mint-green powdery eye shadows, frosted cotton-candy pink and coral lips, bashful peach and pale berry blushes were the tones of the fair maidens' faces and gowns. I was ushered across the room to cousin LeeLee, who was a lacy white wedding cake, on whose bright red ringlet curls rested a rhinestone-encrusted crown laden with white orchids. She gracefully bent down, puddling her massive skirt to kiss me.

"Sweet thing, what took you so long? We're just about to get up on the float. These are Lisa and Eugenie, my two little attendants, and girls, this is my little cousin Bryan. He's gonna be my special page tonight. So y'all be sweet and play nice."

I grinned, but I don't think the little ruffled girls relished the idea of sharing the Queen's float with anyone else, much less a pink-suited boy. Quiet fell over the room, and all eyes turned to the grand doors, in front of which stood Miss Le Blanc, a portly woman dressed from head to toe in poufs of deep purple silk taffeta, which caused a nearly deafening rustle when she wobbled or gestured. An eggplant of a woman, there was no discerning where her waist resided or if she actually had one. Her noteworthy girth raised the question of whether she wore a hoop skirt or whether this was her actual form. Around her jowly neck was a mammoth cameo on a black velvet ribbon that threatened to get lost in the folds, and in her hand was a tall, ornately carved walking stick festooned with iris and lilacs, which she used to pound on the wooden floor in order to elicit silence. With each hammering thump, some of the tiny petals would tinkle delicately to the ground. She cleared her raspy throat and warbled grandly, "The grand promenade of the Spring Fiesta will soon commence, but before it does, I want to say a few words. Eh-hem, young ladies, please remember that you are just that, ladies, daughters of ladies, granddaughters of ladies, and great-granddaughters of ladies, and so forth. Therefore there will be absolutely no smoking or drinking of any kind, always wear your white gloves, and most

39

important, mind your hoops when you sit so that they don't pop up over your pretty heads, exposing your Southern pride. Now smile your beautiful smiles and enjoy your magical night in old New Orleans. Dammit, Mary-Grace Bienvenue, spit out that gum, you look like a cow chewing its cud, that is just plain backwater trash tacky."

Both of the tall paneled doors of the Pontalba Building opened wide and the procession began, each demoiselle was met by a handsome midshipman in formal white dress, and I trailed dutifully behind LeeLee making sure her diaphanous train was properly flowing and never stepped upon. At first I was nervous, but Jackson Square was ablaze with light, as was the old St. Louis Cathedral, and in an instant we were high atop the tractor-drawn papier-mâché Queen's float. Moozie was right. The pink of my suit was a perfect match to the girls' sashes as well as to the boughs of gargantuan paper roses draping the royal vessel, and I was sure not to disappear against the night sky, for I was placed front and center, like a ship's figurehead. With LeeLee now secure upon her throne, we all basked in the glow of small chasing lights that outlined the perimeter of the float, lending a slight vaudeville quality to the picture.

The marching band struck up a jazzy rendition of "Dixie," and the drums and brass reverberated against the crumbling historic walls of the decadent old quarter, as the rickety procession ambled down St. Peter Street. Smiling, waving furiously, and tossing countless stems of mini-carnations to the sparse crowd, we were on our way. Within moments we passed my fabulous aunts Mid and Vie's wrought-iron balcony on the corner of Royal and St. Peter. They were nurses and wore white uniforms and drank scotch with my parents, and although not related to them by blood, I loved them most. Theirs was my favorite location for Mardi Gras parade grandstanding. Upon first sight, just the height of the antique third-story apartment provoked a dare for float-riding maskers, almost goading them to attempt to reach the lofty balcony with their tossed beads, doubloons, and trinkets. I also loved the fact that for pranks, time and gravity were on my brother's and my side. We could release things overboard from the terrace like grapefruit, shoes, or dog droppings upon unsuspecting pedestrians, and dash inside before detonation.

When I glanced up, there were Moozie, my aunts, Oralea, Dad, and Jay all waving, all smiling, and calling my name. I saw the challenge before me, and I tried with all my tiny might to hurl the carnations, but to no avail. Numerous underhand and overhand attempts were made, but the blooms were not structurally designed to be thrown, rather for cheap corsages and juvenile floral arrangements formed in the shapes of poodles.

Then I heard my brother scream out, *"BRYAN! THROW IT LIKE A SPEAR! THROW . . . IT . . . LIKE . . . A . . . SPEAR!"*

I heeded my brother's advice, and with all the power I could muster, I closed my eyes and javelined a handful of the stalks into the lamplit sky. I was not athletic by any means, but I felt instantly transformed into Super Spring Fiesta Page Boy, able to fling countless boughs of carnations, notwithstanding my slicked hair, satin suit, pink cape, and all. My eyes opened to the sad sight of my empty-handed family. Although initially disappointed, they smiled and waved, and the ladies blew kisses just the same as we forged onward.

Bourbon Street is internationally infamous and synonymous with debauchery. That is fact. Nevertheless, our pretty little pageant turned onto this boulevard of delightful depravity, and I beheld the wanton wonders of such night spots and brothels as Club My Oh My! and The House of the Rising Sun. As we proceeded virtually unnoticed by the drunks, streetwalkers, and drag queens, now at an understandably more accelerated pace than before, my eyes widened and burned with the indelible images of G-string-clad strip-tease dancers bumping and grinding on bar tops as the bouncers tantalized onlookers by flinging the swinging doors open and shut. Each gesture, from every lug on the block, released a different vision, each with its own appropriate deafening musical accompaniment. Above one of the dives was a mechanical swing on which sat a pair of high-heeled, fishnet-hosed mannequin legs, and to the beat of the jazz they would swing out through a hole in the structure over the street revelers. One of the attendants whimpered, covering her eyes, LeeLee was laughing hysterically, and I stood at the center, mouth agape, trying to take in every last marvelous detail of this divine degeneracy, until the procession came to an abrupt halt. Due to the glare from the lights, I couldn't tell if our tractor had stalled or its driver had slunk into a bar to quench his thirst.

Little by little we were now getting noticed by the

tawdry onlookers, who, attracted to the float like mice to cheese, asked what was going on or slurred requests for a carnation. From the back of the growing crowd emerged a swirling band of tripping hippies. They were poster children for the Flower Power era; they actually made Janis Joplin look sober. The leader of the group, complete with a beaded headband and a painted peace sign on his cheek, raised a big gallon jug of Boone's Farm wine and shouted, "Long live the Queen, long live the Queen, a toast to the Queenie."

With that, he downed a huge swig of the wine, and his cohorts cheered him on,

"Now, Queenie baby, it's your turn to drink, we drank to you, you drink to us, it's only fittin', it's only right, it's democratic, baby!"

Remembering Miss Le Blanc's stern regulations, LeeLee tried every excuse under the sun to graciously avoid the invitation. She had a cold that she didn't want them to catch. She was allergic to red wine. But the Mamas and the Papas would have none of it.

"Come on, Queenie, don't be all stuck-up like that. You think you're better than us, just cuz you're wearin' a crown up there on that float and all? DRINK, DRINK, DRINK!"

Now the rest of the expanding mob started to chant along, rocking the float, escalating our fears. I was praying that the float would start to move, but no such luck. The chanting grew louder and louder, then LeeLee stood.

"Bryanny boy, be a dear and hand me the wine."

In shock I stepped toward the lip of the float to get the

decanter. The head hippie handed it to me, saying, "Here you go, Pinky boy. Ooh, fancy-ass cape, man!"

Handing her the oversized jug, I asked frantically, "LeeLee, what are you doing? Miss Le Blanc said absolutely no drinking!"

She stared at me as if to say, *Silly six-year-old, I'll take my chances.* And that is precisely what she did. LeeLee leaned forward to me and confided, "We don't know what these drugged-up crazy kooks might do if I don't take a little sip of their hooch, and I'd rather take a teeny sip than run the risk of them throwing the wine at me and staining my lovely gown and having to deal with your Nan-Nan or big Miss L.B."

That being said, she raised the jug up into the sky, and proceeded to chug what seemed to be the remaining vino. To the ecstatic applause of the crowd, she plopped back down onto her throne and her hoop flew straight up into the sky, revealing her rows upon rows of lace-trimmed pantaloons. Now the cheers were deafening.

After returning the wine, LeeLee swore us all to secrecy just as I'd been sworn to silence before, and I wondered for a brief moment who would really give a damn, the parade was almost over, and she was the Queen, for God's sake. This time the dirty words came to mind, but not out of my mouth. It made sense to remain silent in order to avoid the remote possibility of scandal or the wrath of the eggplant woman. The tractor jolted, almost throwing us from the float, as we continued on what had become a tiring journey.

The remainder of the festival was a blur of half-smiling,

waving strangers in the wonderland that is our French Quarter, and by the time we returned to Jackson Square, the glamorous floodlights and bunting-draped grandstands were gone. A sole saxophonist wailed a sorrowful refrain. A gentle, misty rain began to fall. Dad met us with an umbrella and a plastic go-cup from the corner bar, still looking as dashing as when I last saw him on Aunt Mid and Aunt Vie's balcony, and assisted the royal party with our disembarkment. He bowed and gestured with astounding poise and charm, considering the overwhelming amount of scotch he'd ingested so that he could withstand the evening's silliness. LeeLee kissed me farewell, and the others were met by their parents and escorts for the ongoing festivities. Mom was en route to the midnight supper dance where Dad would reunite with her after delivering me to my aunts' apartment for the night.

An exhausted little monkey, I staggered and swayed much more than my father did as we tried to make our way down the dark, glistening street, and at one point he was forced to steady me from toppling over with his strong guiding hand. When we finally reached the archaic Spanish-arched doorway, he ever so gently turned me to face him, and our eyes met as they had before, although mine were now weary, his glossy and patent-leather black. Laying his large hands upon my slim shoulders, he just stared at the ludicrous sight of his rose-caped son, shook his head, and sighed a deep, long breath of scotch, just as before. Hugging me, he whispered softly in a hushed tone I'd never heard before, "Son, I have got to take you fishing."

Hoop Skirt Doctor

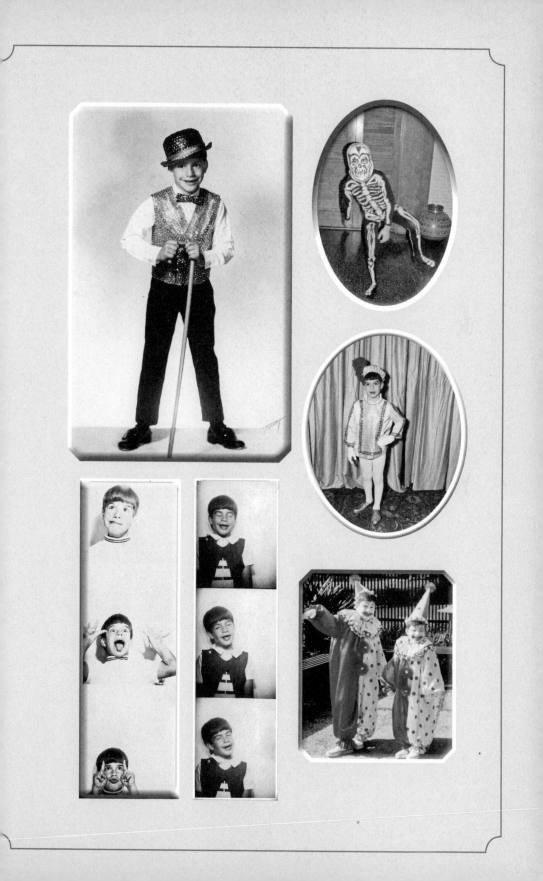

VERY NEAR MY seventh birthday, my secret hoop-skirt fascination was exposed, surprisingly with no fireworks, embarrassment, or shame. At one of my parents' cocktail parties, during an audible lull in the conversation and Herb Alpert, I waltzed wistfully into the smoke-filled Danish Modern living room to the center of the white Flokati rug, wearing the hoop skirt, my favorite blanket fashioned into a waist-cinching sash. Strategically clipped atop my moppish head was mother's *Jezebel*-inspired sausage-curls fall. Clearly I had a thing for hoop skirts. My parents had already begun to suspect something.

First, I did not partake in rough-and-tumble play. In fact, to avoid sports entirely, I frequently spent gym class on a cot in the school nurse's office, complaining of a headache, tummy ache, or arthritis. It wasn't that I completely loathed football; I just thought it ridiculous for seven-year-olds to emulate mammoth men who savagely tackled each other and hurled oddly shaped balls at each other in a game that fitfully started and stopped. But to this day, my brother is convinced that my issues with football stem from an early Saints half-time show at the old Sugar Bowl stadium on Tulane's campus. The tableau was a re-enactment of the War of 1812, complete with historic costumes and real cannons, muskets, the whole nine yards. At one point an antique cannon malfunctioned and blew off the left hand of one of Jean Laffite's aiding pirates, right in front of my eyes. From then on the only part about football that remotely interested me was the miniskirted cheerleaders, but unfortunately they didn't attend the first-grade scrimmages.

Second, I was enthralled with musical comedy. I'd yet to witness a Broadway, national tour, regional, stock, community, or even dinner-theatre production, but I had discovered my mother's collection of original-cast recordings in our den and would play them on the hi-fi at full volume and sing and dance along to Ethel Merman belting out "Rose's Turn" from *Gypsy,* a sight I'm sure would have disturbed its creators, Arthur Laurents and Jule Styne. I am convinced that there is a gene that is triggered in some of us upon hearing the first few notes of any tune by Rodgers and Hammerstein or Lerner and Loewe, causing an irreversible rapture with all things Broadway. The same gene must exist for the sporting sort, and is triggered upon witnessing a first touchdown or home run; it's just much less theatrical. I have to admit there is something wonderfully disconcerting about a prepubescent boy lip-synching with full emotion, tears streaming down his face, the Sondheim lyrics "Mama's gotta move, Mama, mmmmama . . . Mama . . . Mama's gotta let go," or even better any song from "Judy at the Palace."

Third, I had asked Santa for an Easy Bake Oven. That, plus my cocktail-party performance, pushed the envelope to Cleveland. Off to the child psychiatrist I went. My mother sweetly explained, "Sweet pea, now when you meet Dr. Sugar, just talk to him like you would to me or any of your friends, and he will be able to help you, and remember, there's nothing you can't tell him, there's no reason to be embarrassed or ashamed, but you must be strictly honest with him or it doesn't work."

"What doesn't work, Mom? Why do I have to go see Dr. Sugar? I don't feel sick."

"No, of course you're not sick, peanut. Dr. Sugar is a psychiatrist, that's a doctor for the brain and emotions. He will help so you won't have bad dreams anymore."

"But I haven't had a bad dream in weeks."

"Now, pumpkin-eater boy, just go in and talk with him, he's a nice man, I believe that psychiatrists are like God's little angels here on earth, sent to help us with our problems so we don't have to worry Him so much, being that He is so busy with integration and the war and all. I would never ask you to do something that I did not believe was best for you. In fact, can you keep a secret?"

"Uh-huh."

"Well, your brother went to one a few times, and I still do. Now how about them apples?"

"What about Daddy?" I asked.

"Never you mind about him, he wants you to go, too." She bent down and took me into her gentle arms, cupped my face in her polished hands, and looked deeply and lovingly into my eyes and said, "Okey-dokey?"

"Okey-dokey!" And I went every Monday for the next three years, until I was "fixed."

DR. SUGAR'S OFFICE, which was to become my Monday after-school stop, was a modified whitewashed shotgun-style structure with forest-green shutters. Like many of the old homes on the river side of Magazine Street, they were called shotguns because if you fired a shotgun through the front door, the shot would pass through every room before it exited through the back door. In other parts of the country, similar constructions were simply dubbed "railroad flats."

An unassuming faux-wood name plate on the last door toward the rear read DR. MAX SUGAR. The waiting area was a long hallway with Naugahyde sofas from Sears, low-pile brown industrial carpeting, and back issues of *Highlights* and *Time*. At the far left was the door that led to the adults' therapy room, and on the far right was the one for children, and after a few minutes the latter opened to release a grumpy blond boy who shot me a hateful stare to which I returned my signature silly grin. As he exited, he glowered back at me and snarled, "Asshole."

Missing the interaction, Dr. Sugar ushered me into the dull children's room. Against the dingy beige back wall were waist-high shelves with worn games and ravaged books; on the opposite end was a large roll of drawing paper. In the corner were a box of costumes and an open-floor-plan doll house equipped with pliable rubber dolls obviously representing mommies, daddies, brothers, and so on. These did not remotely resemble the glamour of

Barbie or Madame Alexander. I wondered what these sad dolls did to deserve such an existence, torn clothes, misshapen bodies, and no roof over their dented heads. Obviously they were all visitors from the Island of Misfit Toys. Unfamiliar with the surroundings and the custom of child therapy, I timidly took a seat across from Dr. Sugar at the only table in the room.

"Well, Bryan, what we do here is play and draw, but mainly we talk. Is there anything that you'd like to say or do?"

My eyes wandered for a moment, glanced across the room, and were magnetically drawn in the direction of a large costume box. The radiant glimmer of tarnished sequins whispered to me, "Put me on, wear me now, you know you want to, you know you want it!"

Before I knew it, a tutu was around my waist, and shimmery fairy-princess wings were pinned to the back of my striped knit shirt; the tattered daddy doll was sitting on the table in front of me as Dr. Sugar set up the checkerboard. After one or two games, I would rip a piece of the paper from the big roll and draw, draw, draw. That was to be the basic scenario over the course of the next few months; the costumes would vary depending upon my whimsy and mood. Some days a clown; others, Maria von Trappe. The constant, however, was the drawing and the checkers. The good doctor never let me win; he played a fair game and taught me well the rules and strategies of checkers. Although I had no clue why I was dressing up, drawing, and playing checkers with this man, I actually enjoyed our visits. He was a calming influence, an even-keeled person with a soft but gravelly voice, without an overly masculine bravura, just a man.

One October afternoon, after my weekly session with Dr. Sugar, Mother, late as usual, retrieved me from in front of the weathered shotgun, with my brother in tow; we raced to my grandmother's home on St. Charles Avenue to have quick po'boy sandwiches for dinner from Steven and Martin's restaurant across the street, before heading on to church for the Fall Fair rehearsal.

Every autumn, Moozie would put together a small talent show for our church's tiny Fall Fair. Basically it was a recital of old dance routines she had staged in her heyday, usually to recordings of "Alley Cat" or "Hey, Look Me Over." She would kindly find a place for anyone who wanted to participate in the review as long as they followed her strict rules of practicing and punctuality. Unfortunately, much to her chagrin, her immediate family was usually remiss in both. Once in the church recreation hall, Moozie took the young group to a separate area to practice. Moozie's fabulous sister, Aunt Norma, who dyed her hair blond and wore pantsuits, took the adults to another room, and Mom and I, along with my beautiful cousin Donna-Gayle—or D-G as she was called—went to the nursery-school room to rehearse our special secret dance.

D-G was the eldest of the grandchildren and had the best blond flip hairdo, like Elizabeth Montgomery in *Bewitched,* with whom she was often compared. In 1970, that was a huge compliment. I loved the fact that she dug rock-'n'-roll music, that she dressed fashionably mod, and that her skirts were a little bit shorter and her heels a little bit higher than the other girls'. She worked at New Orleans' finest department store, D. H. Holmes, on Canal Street, and it showed.

Entering the Jackson Avenue Evangelical Church of Christ's nursery school, I felt nostalgic. Strange that a first-grader would have nostalgic feelings; however, I did. But there was work to do. Our dance number was to be the big finish, and it had to be a smash. Once again I was sworn to secrecy so that the special effects would have maximum impact on the audience. D-G and I were to dress up as skeletons and do a comic routine to Mancini's theme from *The Pink Panther.*

I loved the concept, and was thrilled to have the privilege of starring in the big finale with my cousin, but there was more, much more—the costumes. An artist friend of my dad's agreed to paint the masks and black leotards with fluorescent paint and to place three large blacklights at the lip of the stage so that when we were illuminated, all the audience would see was dancing bones. Consumed with excitement, I found it hard to concentrate on the steps even though they weren't that hard, just a lot of flap-ball-changing and heel-step-shuffle-stepping. The best use of the glow-in-the-dark effect was sure to be when we lifted off our large skull masks and tossed them back and forth.

After quite a while we took a needed break. Donna lit a long Virginia Slims menthol, and she suggested while inhaling, "Nan Nan, we ought to jazz up this number a bit, don't you think? I mean some of these steps are just a little . . ."

"Square," I chimed in.

"Exactly," D-G agreed, with an explosion of mint-scented smoke. Fanning the smoke away, she continued, "I just saw the most fabulous movie, *Cabaret*, starring Liza Minnelli, who was fantastic, and it was directed and choreographed by Bob Fosse. They did these really cool steps like this . . . and this . . . and this!"

She demonstrated all the sexy, hip-popping signature movements of Mr. Fosse, each step growing more raucously bump-and-grind than the juicy one before. Epiphany. Once again I had a calling. I couldn't sit still, I had to try it, so I joined in with Donna and shimmied, pelvis-thrusted, and gyrated my heart out, until Mom gently stopped the phonograph and tilted her head.

"Sweethearts, I have to remind y'all that we are still in a church, so let's tone the Fosse down. Now you know Moozie will never go for that style of dancing. Okay, maybe the shimmy and sexy walk, but Donna, honey, she'd never let you do all that hip-shaking in front of the congregation, much less Reverend Murphy."

"But Nan-Nan, you've got to see this movie, I know you saw the Broadway show a few years ago, but the film is a blast. Bryan would love it, it's got all those great show tunes and Joel Grey as the Emcee, and if Liza Minnelli doesn't win the Oscar, well, something's wrong with the world. Why don't you take Bryan to see it? It's all singing and dancing, you'd flip, let's all go, I'd love to see it again myself!"

Nothing in the world was going to stop me from seeing *Cabaret*. Nothing. So I glanced upward to heaven, stared at the portrait of the Savior above me, and quickly and solemnly prayed for divine intervention and permission to make the pilgrimage. As I blinked, he seemed to nod, smiling his approval. My eyes slowly descended from the apparition and focused upon another, more tangible deity in maternal form.

"Mother, please take me. I've got to see *Cabaret,* I'll die if I don't, please take me, oh mama, pleeease!" This was to be my mantra, until she acquiesced.

Smiling softly and shaking her coiffed head, Mother calmly explained to us that some of the show's subject matter was most definitely inappropriate for a young boy on the verge of seven, especially the blatant promiscuous S-E-X, and especially the blatant H-O-M-O-S-E-X-U-A-L-I-T-Y references. Furthermore, she explained, I was more of a *Mary Poppins* or *Sound of Music* kind of boy. But Donna sweetly assured Mom that all that S-E-X stuff would fly over my head—which was true—and I would really dig all the singing and dancing and big, splashy musical numbers.

Over the course of the coming weeks we wore down Mom's resistance to the movie and the new moves for our skeleton dance. I even solicited the support of Dr. Sugar. When Mom would frequently excuse herself to the "little girl's room" to "tinkle," D-G and I would run our bawdy alternative steps. She would show me what Joel Grey did in the film, and then she would emulate Liza.

"Bryanny boy, let's take it from the bridge, and hip, hip, shoulder-roll back, eight-ball corner pocket, and bump it to the other side. Man, I tell you, it's going to be a gas doing these sexy moves for all those uptight churchy folks, and when we break out all loosey-goosey and go to town during the funky section, they are going to get so bent!"

I loved the groovy way she spoke, and often tried to incorporate some of her hip words, such as "funky," into my everyday vocabulary. She never treated me as less than an equal, never as a little boy. I wished that she were my sister.

I suppose our nagging, in conjunction with Dr. Sugar's input, finally wore her defenses down, for Mom finally informed us that after Sunday school and Sunday brunch at Moozie's, we would all go see *Cabaret* together. Thus the seemingly endless countdown began.

Rehearsal after that point was a lost cause, and I was grateful that I only had to wait less than twenty-four hours; otherwise the anticipation would have been unbearable.

EVEN THOUGH IT was mid-October, we sat sweltering in the unseasonable swampy heat in the back of the station wagon, awaiting my habitually tardy mother. Dad rarely accompanied the family to church; he believed that since God was everywhere, he could worship in the comfort of his bed and watch the game until the morning pains subsided, with his personal hangover remedy, a Heineken. Without any warning, a whirling dervish of coral-tinted shantung silk flew into the driver's seat, turned on the ignition, and was met by desperate cries for air-conditioning and our favorite radio station, WTIX.

"Boys, hold your horses, I've got it covered. Now should I go out the interstate, or the back way?"

Jay said, "Mom, take the highway like we always do, it's not a school day so there won't be any traffic. Jesus, Mom! Is there any perfume left in the bottle? I can't breathe, roll down the windows before I have an asthma attack!"

As he started to wheeze, she retorted, "Dawlin' I'm so sorry, but let's not take the Lord's name in vain, especially on His day, He doesn't ask us for much and I think it's the least we can do, to praise His name, not defame it."

"Okay, Mom, but please roll your window down before I die, and step on it, you know how I hate to walk in late."

I was in complete agreement. Walking late into church was most embarrassing, as we were obligated to sit in the front pews with Moozie and my uncles and whatever other family members happened to attend on that particular Sunday.

We were always dressed up in conservative coats and ties, even in the deadly heat of summer. Soon we would develop a frightening seventies style, which, thanks to the God to whom we were about to pray, was short-lived. Fashion plate that she was, Mother's attire was often a bit more outstanding and grand than the rest of the congregation's lesser sense of style. Today she was a vision in coral, with the perfect matching shade of lipstick, tan ostrich pumps, and a matching handbag. I believe that if she could have gotten away with wearing a ball gown to church, she would have done so in a New York second. In her mind, I'm sure it was one of her ways of celebrating God's creation, especially all things pretty. Luckily this tendency toward vanity was entirely offset by her selfless generosity.

We arrived mid-procession of the feeble and deafeningly

off-pitch choir, and had to follow behind them in humiliation to the forwardmost pews, only to be met by the stern stares of Moozie and the rest of her brood. Her exasperation didn't last very long, and she pinched our cheeks and quietly kissed us hello. Under her breath she petulantly asked our mother, "Gayle, can you ever be on time? What was it today?"

"Asthma attack." Mom looked to Jay and winked, and his eyes rolled as he stifled a grin. Moozie abruptly dropped her accusing tone and reached over to pat Jay's thigh.

"Oh, tomato, I hope you're feeling better, because I made you your favorite pie."

"Banana creme?"

"That's right, baby doll, banana creme." With that she leaned back over to Mother and whispered, "Honey, you have an extra cup of coffee at fellowship time, I've got to stop by Gambino's bakery and pick up a banana creme pie."

Church was more unbearably boring than usual. Reverend Murphy was an inspiring, motivating, and extremely handsome minister. He was commandingly tall, with a resonant baritone, and wore a black pompadour coif with cool long sideburns. He resembled an older Elvis, if Elvis had stayed in shape. He was extremely popular with the ladies of the church, but even more so with the men. I rarely understood the sermon at this age, maybe due to the King James translation. It wasn't until years later, when Reverend Murphy introduced the congregation and the growing youth group to a more contemporary version of the Bible called *The Way,* that I was able to comprehend his heated and impassioned preaching. Then

I followed along; I would make sure that my soul would never burn for eternity in hell. But today, no parable or psalm could take my mind off *Cabaret*.

The family brunch at Moozie's after church was typically dysfunctional, but that never diminished Moozie's determination to keep her family united despite its own reluctance. So almost every Sunday we would commune. Holidays such as Christmas Eve, Easter, and Thanksgiving, when tensions would normally escalate, went surprisingly smoothly, as long as my mother did not have to cook. The other family holidays, like the Fourth of July, Labor Day, and Mardi Gras, were disastrous, maybe because the festivities traditionally took place outdoors; my family did much better indoors and near a wet bar. Happily, today was to be free of any turmoil, and soon we were all filled with anticipation, headed for the Lakeside Cinema.

For the last two weeks, whenever we drove past the theatre, I was mesmerized by the giant cutout of Liza Minnelli as Sally Bowles, dressed in her purple halter top, hot pants garter belt, fishnet stockings, derby hat, and huge, spidery eyelashes. And now, with tickets and popcorn in hand, we made our way into the sparsely populated cinema, finding great seats in the center, a whole row to ourselves. It was just D-G, Moozie, Mom, and me. The ladies chattered away about cousin so-and-so's new hairdo, and what they thought of the sermon, until suddenly the General Cinema's signature trailer emblazoned the screen. There would be a few previews, then it began—*Cabaret*.

I was never again to be the same boy I had been when I entered the theatre. The musical numbers were different from any musical movie I'd ever seen, spectacularly raw, frightening, comic, and definitely sexual. I felt a tingle downstairs, the beginning of an erection. Unlike my experience at church, I was never bored watching *Cabaret*. Even though I couldn't understand all of the words, I somehow sensed the emotional life behind them and it carried me through to the next musical sequence. The only sign of trouble came toward the end, when Michael York screams, "Oh, fuck Maximilian."

Then Liza quips back, "I do."

Then Michael York smiles and adds, "So do I."

Audible gasps from Mom, and even louder from Moozie. "That wasn't in the play, in fact there was no Maximilian." Mom looked down at me and said, "Honey, we don't use that word. That's a very naughty word."

She had worked tirelessly at trying to rid me of my foul mouth. Even my father had toned down his vulgar expletives. Now Bob Fosse had put them back in her little angel's head. But I assured her, "Like you told me, Mom, I shouldn't use words that I don't understand."

"That's my sweet little man."

Soon the film was done. While the audience applauded, Moozie huffed and briskly exited our aisle, saying, "I don't see why they can't make more happy movies like they did in my day, not with all that cussing, there's no need for that, it's just common, I'm going to the ladies' room, I'll meet you in the lobby."

Under her breath, Donna whispered to Mother that in Moozie's day, movies didn't have sound yet.

. . .

On monday I came tearing into Dr. Sugar's session room and, without a word, raced to the big roll of drawing paper, ripped off an unusually long piece, spread it on the floor, then lay on top of it, pleading, "Trace me, please, Dr. Sugar, trace me!"

He agreed and traced me, pausing a few times to ask me what this was about and telling me to keep still or the silhouette would not resemble my form at all. Finally, when he'd finished, I jumped up, grabbed the crayons, and proceeded to color on my body's own outline. We talked about why I loved *Cabaret* so much, and how I couldn't understand why my father had no desire to see it; in fact he said he thought the Broadway show was stupid. And I said how I thought football was stupid.

As we discussed my feelings, a seed of understanding was planted that would help me later on. Basically, he helped me to see that my father and I were complete opposites; it didn't mean that he loved me any less. We were just different. Dad and Jay were football and sports; Mom and I were theatre and fashion, and that was all right. All men didn't have to like sports. In fact, Dr. Sugar said that he really didn't care for football whatsoever.

At the end of our session my masterpiece was complete. Upon my traced form I had drawn a purple halter top, hot pants, garter belts, fishnet stockings, a derby hat, and big spidery eyelashes just like Liza.

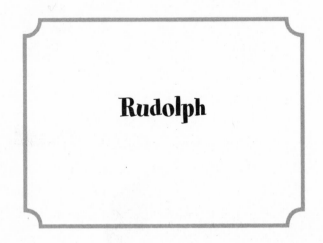

Rudolph

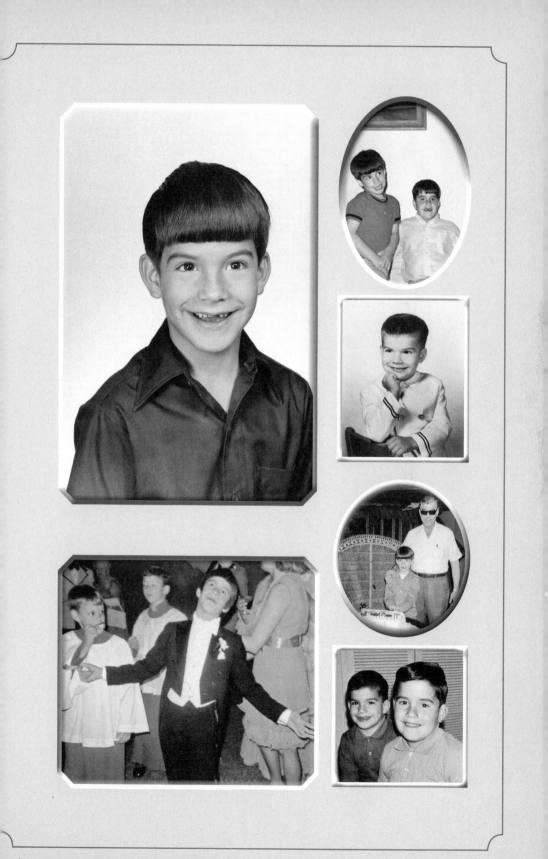

"**B**RYANNY BOY, you are just not concentrating, it's flap-step, step, shuffle-step, ball change, then hop-hop-hop. Got it? O-kay, from the top . . . Gayle, play the record . . . five, six, seven, eight . . ."

Moozie and her sister Norma were seated in the armed Danish Modern dining chairs upholstered in turquoise bouclé, both wearing cat-eyed glasses, with their legs crossed at the ankles, and both fiercely watching my every move. They were, after all, the famous Nuss sisters, founders of the Nuss School of Dance. At the tender ages of twelve and fourteen, they had been put to work teaching dance by their mother, Grandma Katie, who I'm told made "Mama Rose" look like a wallflower. Their first revue at the French Opera House was a smashing success, and to this day I am stopped on the streets of New Orleans by elderly women who recall that Miss Nuss taught them how to dance as well as to be ladies. Norma retired after marriage, but helped Moozie when she was needed.

The word *partiality* was and still is used often in my extended family. Katie was partial to Norma, Moozie was partial to Gayle, but what could have torn the sisters apart made them closer despite the shortcomings of their parents. Norma was everything to Katie, but Moozie was the daughter who cared for her until her dying day. When confronted by this rampant favoritism, Moozie just shrugged, eyes raised to the sky, saying, "You can't help who you love."

Although the famous Nuss sisters were the closest of siblings, they were very different. Moozie, whose nickname often varied, but always contained the syllable "moo," was large and loathed anything to do with cooking. Norma was thin and a gourmet. Hazel had let her hair turn silver, and dressed conservatively. Norma was a bottle blonde who was the first to bob her hair and become a flapper in the 1920s, and now the first to wear a ladies' pantsuit. But both felt unswerving love and devotion to their family. Aunt Norma called me "heart." She taught Sunday school and always made sure to include Jay and me when her class made holiday presents so that my parents would always receive something handmade from us.

The Nuss sisters were here to assess and perfect Mom's choreography for my third-grade spectacle. The music started, and the strains of "Rudolph the Red-Nosed Reindeer" reverberated through the room as I started tapping across the gray terrazzo floor, slipping every so often because of the high polish and wax buildup. That didn't stop me. I was Rudolph, the soon-to-be star of the third-grade Christmas play, *The Night Before Christmas.*

Now, you may be saying to yourself, there is no Rudolph in *The Night Before Christmas*. Well, let me tell you there was going to be one in the Henson Auditorium on December 18, 1971, for two performances only! My teachers had noticed my spark of theatricality and created this part just for me. Now that I had Moozie and Norma to guide me professionally, and the promise of a lit-up red nose, this performance was going to slay all of Isidore Newman School. Newman is one of the most respected private college preparatory learning institutions in New Orleans and the entire Mississippi Delta region. It's alumni is a who's-who of New Orleans, and since my father attended until he was sent to Culver Military Academy, he insisted that Jay and I would be Newman Greenies.

The third-grade Christmas play (yes, it was still called a Christmas play) was one of the big three events of the year, along with the fifth-grade play and the high school musical. Three years before, Jay had made a respectable Frosty. Now I, the singing and tap-dancing Rudolph, was poised and ready to go down in grade-school theatrical history. But how? The dance was good, but secretly I wanted *great*. My Rudolph needed to be as good as the Ernie Flatt dancers on *The Carol Burnett Show*. As I was tapping, flapping, and ball-changing my heart out, Mom stopped the routine.

"This number needs something with more pizzazz, something show-stoppy, something acrobatic. Baby, can you do a cartwheel?"

"Of course I can, Mom."

Challenged, I started to prepare to do a cartwheel and

all was going fine, the jump, each hand perfectly placed, legs straight and toes pointed, but what neither one of us realized was that because of the metal taps and highly buffed stone flooring, I had no hope of a smooth landing. I slid across the floor and careened into Aunt Norma, causing her to collide into Moozie, sending her hot cup of Sanka flying. At this point it occurred to all of us that this trick was not a viable addition to my performance. Unbeknownst to us, Dad, with scotch number three in tow along with Jay, had been spying on our rehearsal during a commercial break, and my flailing fall sent him into peals of laughter.

"Encore! Mr. Astaire!" he shouted. And Jay said, "Smooth move, Ex-Lax."

Norma was at first shocked by the display and by the sight of her sister dripping in Sanka, but instantly she joined the chorus of laughter. Soon Moozie, too, joined in.

The only person not laughing was Mom. Holding back her own giggles, she noticed the tears forming in her little deer's eyes. She tried to explain that no one was laughing at me, but with me, and that my wonderful pratfall was just as good as Dick Van Dyke and those comedians I loved to watch on TV.

"Baby dear, you are very talented and are a natural comic, that's why everyone is laughing." Then, to Jay and Dad, "Okay, you two, cut it out, I bet neither of you two galoots can do that or have any better suggestions." Jay snorted, "I don't know, Mom, but the best part was the upside-down landing. Dad, the game!"

With that they bolted to the den, shut the door, and were glued to the tube for the duration.

Norma and Moozie joined Mom in reassuring me as we got back to the task at hand. They agreed that future rehearsals were closed to anyone but us, the artists. The music started, the flapping and ball-changing followed, and when I arrived at the dance break, the very place where the ill-fated cartwheel was to be, I stopped and, without knowing what else to do, stood on my head. In an overwhelming response, my artistic directors exclaimed, "That's it!" "Now we're cooking!" "Hot diggedy!"

Mom flew to my side and, like a swan, enfolded me in her wings. "See my little red-nosed reindeer, see what you can do? Now let's perfect it."

For the next hour, my terpsichorean muses created extensive leg choreography while I was performing the headstand. Legs together, right leg extends, left leg extends, both together, and then clap the feet to the beat. This new addition was a surefire show stopper, and every night for the next two weeks after my homework was done, we drilled the routine, sometimes with Moozie and Aunt Norma, but primarily it was just Mom and me, fine-tuning the dance.

The school year for a mother must be quite taxing, playing chauffer, disciplinarian, chief cook and bottle washer, and spiritual guide, but now mine was also obsessed with figuring out how the light-up nose would (a) work and (b) remain on my face. Mom's brother, Uncle Dick, was talented with a hammer. He could hang paintings and artwork to perfection, and anything electrical as well as small carpentry tasks were his specialty, but my light-up nose baffled him. So never able to accept defeat until every possible avenue was explored, Gayle contacted the head electrician at Pontchartrain Beach. "The Beach" was my father's family business, and, obviously, there were a few perks. If Mr. Gephardt could make the multicolored lights chase in myriad formations all over every thrill ride of the park, even with missing fingers, he could create an illuminated red nose for a third-grader.

Some of his early attempts with an extension cord were beyond disastrous, but finally, just a few days before the performance, he rigged a battery pack that worked. My mother thought that if someone could create an entire light-up costume for the stripper character of Electra in *Gypsy,* a Rudolph nose should be a cinch. And he did it! Inside the very shiny red clown nose was nestled a small Christmas tree light. The wires were fitted around the front of my face, attached to tight-fitting, crescent-shaped behind-the-ear metal eyeglass frames. The dark wires were then disguised and woven through my antler headdress, designed by Miss Inez, then to a battery pack for which the on-off switch was in my pocket.

Another pressing issue was how the antlers could be constructed so as not to be crushed or broken during the big trick. Trial and error proved the best system for determining what fabrics and supports to use. The final result was black felt-covered wire similar to the type used for a Slinky, so that the antlers could bend but return to their original shape. Every last detail was taken into consideration; even the wires that went across my face were painted by Norma to match my skin tone. There was a motto in our family: If you are going to do something, do it right! The underlying and unspoken message was "pull out all the stops and take no prisoners."

The day before the dress rehearsal at school, the *grandes dames* of dance convened in our extravagantly decorated Christmas home. This year Gayle went overboard, with all my support, as we both loved decorating for every holiday. We often joked that guests must always be in constant motion, because if someone sat too long, Mom would affix a red velvet bow to them. The chairs were in place, the record on the hi-fi, poised for playing. As was the drill, the ladies sat, legs crossed at the ankles, all smiles, their colorful rhinestone Christmas brooches gleaming as the tree lights across the room glistened in the facets. Norma's was a modern golden angle with a starburst diamond halo. Moozie's was an elegant emerald-and-ruby tree. And Mom's, which was a gift from Norma, was a bust of Rudolph with a big ruby for the nose. I hid in the study, assembling my brown polyester and corduroy ensemble, and trying desperately to get the nose and antlers on right. Finally I had to call Mom in for assistance, and as she adjusted the venison-inspired regalia, I noticed the brooch.

"Mom that is so beautiful."

"Your sweet Aunt Norma gave it to me, I Sewanee she is so thoughtful. Okay, mister love bug, now don't forget to use your clicker to turn the light in your nose on and off, and remember you are special. Just like Rudolph can light up the sky, you can light up the stage."

She gave me a gentle kiss on my forehead, and as I looked at myself in the mirror, I thought to myself, *I am Rudolph and I will play in the reindeer games*. Although I looked like a living TV antenna, I could only see Rudolph the young buck. Mom peered grandly out in front of the walnut study doors and announced, trying to imitate a heralding bugle, "Ta-ta-ta daaaaaa, ladies, I give you Rudolph, the Red Nosed Reindeer!"

The music started, and I was flapping and tapping my heart out, turning the nose on and off, getting applause and cheers from my beloved audience of three. As the routine grew, with Moozie's suggested key changes to heighten the excitement, my showbiz gene kicked into full throttle, and I was flying, but forgetting to turn off my very shiny nose. By the time I arrived at the headstand, inebriated with performing, I smelled something burning.

"AUGHHHHHH, GET IT OFF!" I cried, yanking the contraption from my face, revealing my own blistered red nose. Suddenly I felt so stupid, this whole thing was stupid, and to top it all off, my nose was ruined.

In the panic, the ladies rushed to my side, scurrying me into the kitchen to get the burn salve, arguing over the latest first-aid treatment for burns. Just then, Dad burst through the den door.

"Jesus Christ, what the hell is going on in here?"

"Johnny, it's all right, we have it under control, Bryanny's nose got burned a little during the dance, that's all. Baby dear, I am so sorry, does it hurt much? You don't have to wear the light-up nose if you don't want to."

"Oh, let me see." Dad took my rattled little face into

his big hands and announced, "Looks like you'll live, son. But a word of advice—scrap the light-up nose, you don't need it." Dad gave me a wink, and then came back with, "Any of you ladies care for a cocktail? I'm bellying up to the bar."

"John, really, another?"

There was a peculiar silence completely foreign to our home during their steely stares.

Norma was first to break the chill. "Johnny, sweetie, I'd love a highball." Moozie chimed in with a request for a Brandy Alexander, and of course Dad knew what Mom always drank. She smiled insincerely, and a Chivas Mist with a twist was added to the tab. Dad produced a triumphant grin and stumbled ever so slightly, enough that only Mom would notice, as he threw aside the swinging kitchen door and bellowed, "Jaybird, get out the shaker and the ice crusher, and bring out the hooch." He turned back to catch Mom's glare, and there was no trace of a grin remaining on his face, but only an expression of contempt. Then he let the door close, flapping back and forth, as we all stood in silence.

"Well, hell's bells," Norma said, trying to break the awkwardness of the moment, "this child needs some ice." And in a flash she produced an impromptu dish-towel ice pack. "Now, heart, put this on your boo-boo nose and rest in the living room, and maybe go over the routine in your head, and we'll be right out."

The three women watched as I made my exit, but instead of resting in the living room, I sat near the door and put my ear against it just like on *I Love Lucy*.

"Gayle, what is going on? Why is Johnny drunk in the middle of the week?" Mom was a dam about to break. She took a deep breath with the hope of buying time to come up with a respectable answer, but there was none. Moozie continued, "Maybe it's not all that bad; he is a good provider."

With that, Mom broke down. I could hear crying.

"My God, Gayle, get ahold of yourself, it will be okay, tell me what he has done," said Moozie. "Has he hit you? 'Cause if he has, I will knock his lights out."

Then Mom spoke softly through intermittent gasps. "No, he hasn't hit me, he would never do that. He just drinks all the time, from the minute he gets home till he goes to bed or passes out, whichever comes first. Everything is my fault. He blames me for it, and all I've done is try to be a good wife and mother. He barely has time for the children. He's plastered by seven-thirty. Jay wants so much to play with him or do homework with him and be a good son for him, and he doesn't even know Bryan. That child is scared of him. Scared of his own father. We never know what mood the scotch will put him in. Some nights he's actually fun, but on some he's a horror."

"Well, you've just got to put your foot down and tell him that you will not put up with his shenanigans anymore, now march right in there."

"Mother, you don't understand, Dr. Waters says it's a disease, that he is sick."

"Baloney sausage! And please don't tell me you are still seeing that psychologist, you are not crazy."

"No, I assure you I'm not crazy now, but I'm getting

driven there and fast, and Dr. Waters is one of the finest psychiatrists not psychologists in the entire city of New Orleans."

"Psychiatrist, psychologist, it's a bunch of hooey. Why do you always have to go see a doctor and tell other people, complete strangers, your problems? This is a private family matter. In my day we didn't just go air our dirty laundry to any Tom, Dick, or Harry. Is this the same doctor that put Jay on the Ritalin drug? The child was just being a boy and—"

"Mother, this is not helping at all. The fact is that Johnny's doctor—" And before Moozie could utter another word, Mom quickly continued, "His cardiologist—" That silenced the room entirely.

Norma, who had remained silent throughout the heated exchange, knew when and when not to interfere, and now was the perfect moment to interfere. In the most calming of tones, she tried to calm the battling mother and daughter. "Gayle, dear, I thought John's heart was all right. That scare a few years ago was only a scare, right, sweetie? Isn't that what you said? Honey?"

Mom started to speak, but uncharacteristically faltered.

"No one, myself included, but especially Johnny's daddy, wanted to believe big, strapping John Batt had a heart attack, not the son of Harry J. Batt Senior, founder of Pontchartrain Beach!"

"Now, Gayle I will admit he can be a bit much," Norma chimed in, "but would he really . . . "

"At thirty-five years old he had a myocardial infarction,

which, as you remember, kept him in the hospital for a couple of weeks. Harry thought that by calling it by its technical name, it would lessen the stigma of a heart attack, which in reality it was," Mom said. "Dr. McCurley said that it was nothing to fool with, and John should cut down on salt and drinking, and quit smoking, none of which he has done. Oh yes, he did switch to Heineken for a year, but he was back on J&B in no time."

Moozie exclaimed, "Well, dear, you are his wife, you just have to make him. I would never have tolerated this sort of behavior from your father, or from any man for that matter."

"Mother, you can't 'make' anyone 'do' anything. Dr. Waters said that all I can do is change myself and how I deal with it, that's part of Al-Anon."

"They meet at my church," Norma added. "Isn't that for . . ." She suddenly lowered her voice to a whisper. ". . . alcoholics?"

"No, Aunt Norma, it's a group for the spouses of alcoholics."

Moozie announced, placing a hand above her bouffant, "I have had it up to here. John is not an alcoholic, and you are not going to meetings and telling complete strangers he is. I don't give one iota what this Dr. Waters says, it's not proper."

"Well, Mother, *I've* had it up to here," Mom said, placing her hand mockingly at an even higher mark. "I am not sure whether he is or is not an alcoholic. All I do know is that I can't live like this."

Unintelligible as all this was to a third-grader, I knew

something was wrong. The ice for my fried nose had melted away, and just then Jay emerged from the den with the tray of libations, followed by Dad, who quickly dove into the master bedroom. As Jay approached the kitchen door, he signaled for me to open it, which I did with great hesitation. The heated discussion came to an abrupt halt when they gazed at the boy cocktail waiter and Rudolph the Burnt-Nosed Reindeer.

Jay offered the tray to Mom first, saying, "Dad told me to tell you to finish without him. He kept spilling stuff, so he went to bed."

Mom told Jay how gallant he was to bring the drinks to them, and that it was time for bed.

"But, Mom, I get to stay up a half hour longer than Bryan, and *Laugh-In's* coming on."

"All right, Bryanny, time to bathe and it's lights out, okay, angel? Now give Moozie and Aunt Norma a kiss good-bye."

Jay was quick with the kisses and off to the den in record speed. As they bent down to kiss me and pinch my cheeks, offering words of encouragement for tomorrow's performance, I felt as though once again I was privy to top-secret information. This would not be hard to conceal. Finally, Mom hugged me a little longer than usual, whispering in my ear, "Just like Rudolph, you are a very special boy."

THE NEXT MORNING I was awakened by my mother wearing a lace-covered housecoat with a pale blue satin ribbon and a red clown nose clipped to her pale powdered face, gently singing "Rudolph the Red-Nosed Reindeer."

"Pumpkin-eater boy, it's time to get up, today's the big day. If you and Jayzee are extra quick getting dressed, we can stop at Royal Castle for breakfast. When you're ready, come by our room and give your daddy a kiss good-bye."

In a flash we were dressed and waiting by the door.

"Dammit, John, you *have* to go, it's your son's school play. You barely do anything with the boys. You have to, and that is that!"

We knocked in hopes of ending the argument, and Dad told us to come in. He was still in bed, his cigarette glowing in the darkness.

"Come give your Pops a hug and a kiss," he said, and as we did so, smelling the stale scotch on his breath and feeling his scratchy whiskers, he said in a hoarse tone, "How much do you love me?" And as was the drill, mimicking the pose of the funny-faced dime store statue with its arms stretched out wide that we had given him for Father's Day, we said in unison, *"This* much." As I was leaving the dark room, I looked back and asked, "Daddy, are you coming to my play today?" He rumbled, "I'm not sure, sport, but I'll try." I shrugged and started for the door, but turned back as I touched the brushed-nickel doorknob. "Okey-dokey, Pops, but I still love you *this* much."

THE MAIN REASON Mom wanted to stop off at Royal Castle was to kill two birds with one stone. I never understood that expression; either way you end up with two dead birds. The same with catching more flies with honey than with vinegar; you still end up with flies. The short-order cook, Miss Darlene, was always so nice to us, complimenting my mom on her hair or outfit, and she always made the best silver-dollar pancakes. Miss Darlene sported a nearly foot-high, fire-engine-red beehive do, which she would decorate for various holidays, and on this day, flocked sprigs of holly sprang out from the numerous caverns, hills, and dales of her hair. One of Mom's outfits, a groovy multicolored silky raincoat, had been the subject of Miss Darlene's praise. The last few visits, Miss Darlene had been blue about her son in Vietnam, and had thoroughly forgotten to decorate her hair for Thanksgiving. So while going through her closet a few days prior, which was a rarity, Mom noticed the coat. She hadn't worn it much, and thought that since Miss Darlene loved it so, she should have it. At first Mom had second thoughts about giving someone a used coat—it might be considered tacky—so she also placed a pair of season passes to Pontchartrain Beach in the pocket. Mom loved the fact that the business brought so much joy to people of all ages, and even more she loved sharing it with her family and as many people as she could. Dad often said Mom suffered from an identity crisis: she thought she was Santa Claus.

Miss Darlene was ecstatic to receive the coat and the passes. She hugged and thanked Mom profusely, and as we were driving to school in the new Oldsmobile Custom Cruiser, adorned with a big red velvet bow on its front grille, making notes of new, overly decorated homes to visit on our nightly caroling jaunts, I saw Mom brush away a single tear. "Okay, my Mr. Frosty and Mr. Rudolph. 'Jingle Bells'! Dashing through the snow, in a one-horse open sleigh . . ."

THE MOMENT HAD come. Of course there were a few remarks about my singed nose from some of the other third-graders, but backstage I awaited my cue, butterflies churning in my stomach. Then, hearing David Lane, who was playing the Papa in "The Night Before Christmas," say quite loudly yet with an uncommitted tone, "And what to my wondering eyes should appear, but a miniature sleigh and eight tiny reindeer . . . plus one more," I started prancing with the two rows of four boys dressed identically, except for the non-illuminated clown nose, pulling Santa in his sleigh. My music started and the choir section in the orchestra pit began their singing, and I went to town. I smiled and sold the routine to the back row of the Henson Auditorium.

It came time for my headstand, and the entire audience burst into thunderous applause. With every choreographed upside-down foot and leg movement, the crowd went wild. From my reversed perspective, all I could see were lights and smiles, I didn't know what it was, or if it would last, but I loved this feeling. On a reindeer high for the rest of the day, I welcomed the praise of my classmates and teachers. Even Jay made a point of announcing on the school bus home, "How about my brother as Rudolph!" and there was even more applause.

At home, Oralea had said Mom would be coming home

soon, but that I should get a special treat for my "stupendous" performance. When Dad came home, shortly after five, as the orange winter sun was setting over Lake Pontchartrain, he poured his crystal double old-fashioned glass with a more-than-ample serving. Instead of setting up the checkers set as he usually did in the evening, he bellowed for me to come to the den. I guessed he was going to tell me that he couldn't get away from work to see me. Our eyes met, and he beamed. It seemed like an eternity before he spoke, but when he finally did, there was warmth in his voice, a deep timbre that resonated a pure affection. Of course, he had displayed such emotions before, but not like this.

"Son, you were just great up there on that stage today." He shook his head, not knowing what else to say, started to walk away, but turned and added, "Go put on your costume and tap shoes, and that red clown nose."

I was a bit confused. Feeling a little trepidation, I asked, "Okay, but . . . why, Dad?"

"We're going to show your grandfather just how that damn Rudolph dance is done!"

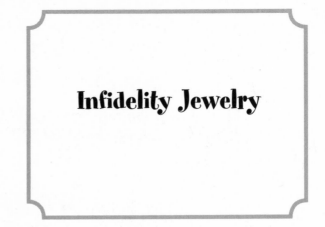

Infidelity Jewelry

IT CAN HAPPEN at any time in a life, in early childhood or late adulthood, but it will happen, the moment when a son or daughter realizes that their parents are human and therefore subject to all human frailties, that the myth of "happily ever after" or even just "ever after" is forced by life itself to crash and burn at some point. As a possible coping mechanism, I feel it's best to straddle the worlds of reality and fantasy, keeping one foot firmly planted in each so that when necessary, one can escape with just a simple shift of weight. The willing of the molecules. The information surrounding my father's short-lived dalliance are sketchy at best. No names or places were ever discussed with me, although mysterious heated arguments were heard from behind closed doors when children were thought to be outside, climbing trees like good monkeys. Only time can heal the inevitable painful realization that our parents are mortal and capable of all human frailties and failings. The wonderings and embellishments of this youthful adolescent's overactive imagination are the following. This is how it all went down in my mind's eye.

THE PHONE CALL was uncannily reminiscent of the call from Norma Desmond to Betty Schaefer at the climax of Billy Wilder's *Sunset Blvd*. Although the names and situation were different, the malicious intent was the same.

"Gayle, dear, do you know where your husband is? Do you know what he does when he tells you he's working late? I thought you'd appreciate my letting you in on his sordid little secret . . ."

Mother had suspected the dalliance, and had some evidence, but nothing concrete until this pivotal moment. Unfairly, any sort of sexual revolution of the sixties had left her in its wake. Years before, Moozie's wedding-night advice was that of her mother and generations before: just lie on your back and pretend to like it. And she did try, but the double standard of the 1950s and her upbringing never allowed for any sexual exploration. "Good" girls just didn't do "that," and "bad" girls didn't get to marry "quality boys." A whole new world of sensuality was exploding all around, but her ears, eyes, and legs had remained firmly closed.

Mother was on the verge of ultimate collapse, but rather than acquiesce to this home-wrecking trollop, she summoned every fiber of her granite Southern ancestors and snapped back with steely grace. "Betty, I hate to spoil your twisted little game, because from the tone of your voice you seem to be enjoying this, but I do know, he confessed last night. Maybe because he sensed that you, given your depravity, would pull such a cruel and common stunt. Let me be crystal clear, he is mine, understand me, and *mine* to deal with. But as for you . . ."

Her voice lowered uncharacteristically, and with calculated articulation she continued as her fevered face reddened and her extremities trembled with rage at what she felt as the most devastating of betrayals.

"Don't ever call my home again, erase this number from your evil sick mind, and when I see your pathetic face anywhere in this city, don't you dare speak to me. You have no right! Go to hell!" With that, she slammed the Princess phone down, actually hoping to hurt the shrew's ears on the other end of the line. *How dare he?* she thought. *How dare he turn me into this whimpering housewife, acting out a sordid soap-opera scenario? How dare he?* Even though the marriage wasn't at its best at the time, how could he ruin whatever chance they had left with a disgusting fling with that dirty tart? She cried to break her heart. She relived every moment leading up to the shattering of her life as she saw it, lists upon endless lists of her devoted, supportive, kind acts. She was clearly wronged and knew it, and she wanted revenge. While contemplating the trauma and agony of divorce, the potential irrevocable impact on her boys, she realized that she somehow, in some way, still loved my father, and bawling like a child, she prayed, "Where were you? How could you let this happen to me? What have I done to deserve this, except try to be a good Christian wife and mother? Goddammit all to Hell!

"Oh, dear Lord, I am sorry, I am so sorry, but I just don't see *why!*"

Suddenly an avalanche of profanity flowed from her. This shocked and terrified her to her very core.

"Now he's got me cursing like him, and to the Lord. Oh, Jesus Christ!"

She cried out louder than a mortally wounded animal, and crumpled to her knees on the marble floor of her beautiful bath suite. "Sweet baby Jesus, forgive me. Help me, please. Lamb of God, Lord, hear my prayer, what do I do? What do I do? What the *hell* do I do?" Gasping in disbelief, she screamed, "This really has to stop!"

She played out the horrors of what a divorce would do to her life as she had come to know it, and that of her cubs. Everything she had ever heard or read reiterated that the worst effect of divorce was on the children, especially at this stage of development. Thanks to the latest round of family counseling, my brother and I were finally somewhat civil. A separation and divorce could ruin everything. Her pumpkins could become potheads or heroin addicts or bums; look what had happened to Art Linkletter's child. Furious as she was, she knew deep in her heart that leaving wasn't an option; she was trapped. Besides, some debris of their love remained, and that single excruciatingly debilitating fact infuriated her even more.

Today her ritual whirlwind of preparation for an outing had a different air. Rather than the usual random flurry into painted perfection, now every move was considered, every effect contemplated. As she tried to outline her full lips, her elegantly monogrammed towel dropped, as did the cherry-toned pencil liner, and she was assaulted with a cruel, unforgivingly reflected glimpse of her now more-than-ample figure.

"Oh my God!" she wailed. "When did I get cellulite, it looks like I've been sitting in cottage cheese!"

Then, in rapid succession, she noticed every minute physical imperfection. With one glance she saw the beginnings of crow's feet. Another look and instantaneously there was a double chin, a roll of back fat, flabby upper arms, and three—no, five—gray hairs. Sadly, the mirror is not a liar, but rather a painfully honest friend, the kind that tells you your husband has been cheating on you and you're getting fat and old. Although still beautiful, she had definitely let herself go.

Assessing her now glaring flaws, she cried out to the mirror, her half-lined lips almost cartoonish against her pale countenance, and grabbing her stomach just above her cesarean scars, she screamed, "Stretch marks! Is this why, John? Is it? Don't like what you see anymore? Sorry, honey, this is what happens when you have two ten-pound boys ripped from your womb!"

Now just plain furious, she slammed her fists on the marble basin, causing a jar of fine translucent power to rocket above her, leaving a trail like a sky-writing airplane overhead, and through her foggy eyes she could see in the mirror that it was spelling out FOOL. The jar suddenly hit the floor, shattering in a mushroom cloud.

Hopelessly reaching for a towel to cover herself, her painted nails grasped like claws on the center of the exquisite hand embroidery that bore her married monogram, the name she accepted upon sacred matrimony. Then, with an unyielding clenched fist, she beat the pale blue *B* on the plush towel as if it were the letter itself that had betrayed her, before crumbling in slow motion to the floor with a flood of tears.

"Miss Batt? Miss Batt? Miss Gayle? You all right?" Oralea asked as she repeatedly knocked on the door. "What is going on in there?"

Oralea pushed the bathroom door the slightest bit open, and it took only a moment for their eyes to meet, and Oralea knew. Her eyes began to fill, but Oralea wisely withheld her tears as her heart broke for her Miss Gayle.

Their sad eyes never broke contact as Oralea consoled her. "Men are men, that's all they are and ever will be. Believe me, Mr. John loves you, you and I both know it. Whatever else is going on, I don't need or want to know about, but I do know this, I been by both your sides since day one, since I served the champagne at y'all's engagement party on Fontainebleau Drive, got you dressed for your wedding, and we ain't giving up, not without one hell of a fight. You hear me, child?"

Mom nodded like a little schoolgirl.

"Now, Miss Gayle, you are going to be fine; let's get you cleaned up, and I'll get this room looking brand new."

She offered her calloused hand to my mother, and helped her to her feet. The stare was finally broken, only to be followed by a desperately weary hug, until the sobbing stopped.

"We got to put ourselves together. I'll call Miss Hazel and Miss Vilma, and they'll be here in a flash. Now, you don't want your mama and sister to see you all bleary-eyed. Remember who you are."

She knew deep in her bones exactly who she was. It was *what* she was at this moment that frightened her so. What she had allowed herself to become, and what she had foolishly allowed others to lead her to be. No more the doormat, no more the good little wife. Gayle stood as tall as she could, arched her back, looked sternly into the mirror, and vowed to her reflection that she would never betray herself or allow herself to be betrayed ever again. With that affirmation freshly and deeply expressed, the hurried process of painting and patching the streaks and puffiness began. Sadly, some cracks could never be covered; there is no creation by Estée Lauder that could ever conceal her shattered heart and broken life.

As she applied a final spray of All Set hairspray to her outdated 'do, the doorbell chimed, startling her. I ran to get the door and greet Moozie and Aunt Vilma. As always, I gave Aunt Vilma two kisses and allowed Moozie to pinch and stretch my cheeks as she referred to me as her "little tomato-eater boy." Even though I was growing up, I loved her babying affection.

Mom entered the room somberly, without her usual flair, and everyone immediately sensed something gravely wrong, including me. Then I realized what it was: Mom and Moozie were wearing the exact same dress! The same matronly polyester jacket and A-line dress!

"Mom! Why are you and Moozie dressed like twins? No offense, Moo, but Mom, you are like how many years younger, and you are dressing just like a grandmother.

Maybe you should go shopping and try something a little cooler."

Oralea scurried me out, telling me that my buddy Chucky had called and to get on my bike and get over to his house. "You go on over by the doctor's house and climb them big oak trees and see if you can see the top of the Zephyr roller coaster when you reach the tippy-tippy top, now get on, I'll take care of everything, go!"

"Okay, okay, I'm going, but Mom, really, you really should think a little more 'now,' it is the seventies, and you're still like kind of pretty."

I was almost out the door when I added, "And hair that actually moved really couldn't hurt, either."

Suddenly the lionesses, with the omission of my stunned mother, instantly joined forces to rush me out, practically placing me on my banana-seat bike and pushing me out the driveway. As I peddled to Chucky's through the labyrinth of lanes that connected the midcentury homes of Lake Vista, I thought more and more about my mother's alarmingly archaic fashion choices. She clearly needed my help, and I knew I had a flair for fashion. I could do this, I thought. I could make over my mom.

The summer before, Jay and I had taken a wild trip up north to tour many different amusement parks with our grandfather Da-Dee, a larger-than-life showman. He was forceful and imposing, with charisma that could illuminate the entire midway. The vacation was amazing, with lots of hotel breakfasts and swimming pools, and the best roller coasters in the country. We stayed with old family friends in Chicago when we visited Marriott's Great America, and I became infatuated with Aunt Gretchen. She had modeled for Coco Chanel in Paris, and currently modeled most frequently for Marshall Field's. *Au courant,* she smoked clove cigarettes from a gold cigarette holder, had cropped jet-black hair and more muted natural-toned makeup with burgundy-lined lips, and everywhere we went, everyone commented on her fabulous style. She knew how to work a look, from top to bottom. Still peddling toward Chucky's, I decided that as soon as I got home that evening, I would find Aunt Gretchen's number and call her for advice. Mom didn't know it yet, but the plan for her full transformation was brewing.

Back at the house, Vilma and Moozie were enraged and torn by the scandalous news. They loved my father, despite his rough edges and his often excessive drinking. He was a kind, generous man. They somehow imagined that it was bound to happen, but the deep gut feeling of "don't fuck with my family" prevailed.

Vilma asked seriously, "Where is he?"

"Not here," Mom replied.

Dad knew he was in serious trouble. To escape the wrath of not just his wife but her mother and sister as well, Dad was hiding at a fishing camp in Lockport, Louisiana. There were three quotes my dad lived by: "The best defense is a strong offense"; "Never bullshit a bullshitter"; and "A hard prick has no conscience." Well, his conscience must have caught up with him this time, as he'd tried to soften the blow by telling all to my mother the night before that fateful phone call. But he'd misjudged Hurricane Gayle, and hoped to ride out the storm from a distance.

Vilma continued, "What are you going to do?"

"Damn men can't keep it in their pants. Do you want a drink, honey?" Moozie inquired.

"No, I want my life back—and, yes, a Chivas Mist with a twist."

"Who doesn't?" Vilma added.

As always, Oralea was one step ahead. The ice had been crushed, the scotch poured, the lemon twist forthcoming. She met Moozie's questioning stare, and handed over the remedy for the mother hen to administer.

Moozie raised an eyebrow as if to suggest that Gayle should dismiss the hired help.

"Mother, please, Oralea knows, she's family. Hell, I bet everyone knows. Johnny and Tommy and their entire crowd have done it; it's like some stupid fraternity. His own father has done it, for crying out loud, and it was mentioned in that *Figaro* newspaper when he was spotted coming out of the House of the Rising Sun on Bourbon Street. But we don't talk about it or dare mention it or dare buy that paper. Boys in Jay's class at Newman were teasing him about it; some tacky parents must have a warped concept of proper dinner conversation or have forgotten about the skeletons dancing in their own closets. When Jay-boy asked Johnny if it was true, he was so furious that he actually couldn't find the words to explain the embarrassment, so he marched Jayzee two doors down and said to Da-Dee, 'Dad, would you please explain to your grandson what this incident is all about?'"

Da-Dee was an extreme presence, a self-made man of considerable wealth and accomplishment. A voracious reader and world traveler, he could converse brilliantly on almost any topic, and he possessed an almost flamboyantly dapper manner of dress and style. A personal favorite of his was the classic black and white houndstooth fabric that adorned his hat, his jacket, and the upholstered roof as well as the bucket seats of his most recent Cadillac. He owned one of the first vanity license plates in Louisiana, which bore his initials HJB-SR. The combination of the houndstooth and the vanity plate were dead giveaways to the *Figaro* reporters, who couldn't help noticing the affectation-mobile parked directly in front of the brothel.

Without any emotion or guilt, Da-Dee sat with Jay and in a matter-of-fact manner, as if he were telling the boy a time-honored adage, stated, "Son, there are just some things you don't ask your wife to do." And that was that.

"Well, I definitely believe in genetics, that's where he got it from; the apple doesn't fall very far from the tree," Moozie quoted.

After a few ample sips, Mother sat up, mustered every bit of strength, and announced, "I don't know how or why, but I don't want a divorce, I don't believe in it. I took a vow, and I will stand by it."

It was at this moment her life changed forever. Some people crumble in the face of betrayal and adversity, but somewhere in her stealthy Southern DNA was the fortitude to survive, no matter what the circumstances. This inner strength would serve her well throughout her life. She realized that she didn't want to be a victim, but rather a victor. Not knowing why or how, Gayle Batt was going to survive.

Moozie, still reeling from the news, said, "Damn it to hell, this is an outrage, we have never had anything like this in our family."

At that, the other three ladies gave Moozie an all-too-knowing look. It was common knowledge that others had stepped out, but of course not her sainted late husband, Dick.

"*Aughhhhh!*" Gayle screamed, shocking all in her presence. "I just want him to hurt like I do. This is not fair. Hell, life is not fair, that's what I keep telling the boys, but this is . . . *shitty*!"

"Gayle, language," Moozie chided.

"Sorry, Mother, but it is. I want to get even . . . not in that way, I could never be unfaithful, or could I?"

"Gayle!" Moozie exclaimed, shocked.

"Mother, you know me. Vilma, you too. I just don't know what to do."

She started to break down, but instantly she forced herself not to cry. Suddenly stoic, she said, "I'll be damned if this is going to get me."

Vilma loved hearing that affirmation. Now, Aunt Vilma always had a wonderfully wicked side; unlike Mom, she could play the game, and her wheels were turning so fast they were audible.

"Sister, I know how to get that SOB where it hurts, in his wallet. If you are sure that this can be worked out, then I say let's scurry downtown, have a delicious lunch at Galatoire's, and then you pillage Adler's."

For generations, Adler's on Canal Street was the preeminent jeweler of New Orleans. The finest and most current as well as classic designs were featured at this Southern treasure chest of gold, diamonds, pearls, and every other precious stone or metal imaginable. Mother nodded softly, and Moozie took her hand in her own gloved one, offering Vilma the other, and they were off to seek bejeweled revenge on the man who had done her wrong.

Before entering Galatoire's, a historic mainstay of cuisine, Moozie whispered to her daughter, "Now, honey, powder your face and fix your lips, you never know who you're going to see here, and I don't want anyone to suspect anything, you just pull your shoulders back, lift that pretty chin and give me that smile, you're going to be fine as wine, just fine."

Gayle came to a halt as she saw the leaded-glass doors that bore the monogram of the famed classic creole restaurant. As she gazed at the entrance, the very place she and John had spent numerous evenings, Vilma knowingly reached for Mom's purse, producing a compact and powder puff, then began the translucent application. Next she gently handed her the frosted coral lipstick, slowly turning the mirror so that Gayle's reflection appeared. She gasped as her eyes started to well.

"Little sister, Mother is right, you have to go in there as if nothing has happened, walk in and smile as if you've not a care in the world. If you can't, we can just go home, but darling, aren't you just craving some delicious oysters en brochette and shrimp rémoulade?"

She grinned as Moozie chimed in, "And some soft-shell

crab and their divine trout meunière almandine. And Bloody Marys all around."

With that she accepted the lipstick, arched her back, lifted her chin, and assumed the traditional mouth formation for applying lipstick. Her top lip stretched widely across, covering her front teeth, and the bottom lip pulled up, covering the bottom teeth, all the while dabbing the pigment with tiny feminine strokes. As soon as she'd finished rubbing the top and bottom lips together, she made a little popping sound as the lips parted.

Vilma produced a lace monogrammed handkerchief. *"Voilà! Blot, s'il vous plaît."*

Gayle replied as the sisters had always done, purposefully murdering the French language, "Mercy buckets."

And together they locked arms, took a deep breath, and just then the doors were flung open for their entrance. Passing the tourists waiting for a seat, Moozie whispered softly in the maître d's ear. He smiled, gesturing the party to follow, "Of course, Mrs. Mackenroth, and how are you and your lovely daughters today?"

"Just ducky, dear."

As they made their way into the heart of the bright tiled and mirrored room, they were greeted by numerous friends and acquaintances; there were smiles and waves and air kisses.

Quickly the busboy brought glasses of iced water and hot French bread, and he was followed by Nelson, who had been our family waiter for generations. Nelson served my grandparents, my parents, and later me. Each family had its own assigned regular waiter. He beamed as he spoke with a hint of a Cajun accent, "Ah, Miss Hazel, and Miss Vilma, and Miss Gayle, how could I be so lucky to have the three most lovely ladies in New Orleans at my table no less, I tell ya, *cher,* my cup she runneth over. So I'm gonna drink from the saucer, now speaking of drinking, what can I get you three for some drinks? Pimm's Cup, Kir Royale, or some Bloodys?"

"Three Bloodys," Vilma ordered, "but make mine gin, Nelson, would you please?"

"Tell me something I don't know. Coming right up. Let me tell you some of the specials. We got a pompano meunière almandine with lump crabmeat on top that is fantabulous, and my favorite, soft-shell crab that are so fresh their little claws are just playing the piano." Nelson demonstrated by dancing his fingers like a crab playing a piano. "And of course we got trout, all the regulars, and your favorite, Miss Hazel, chicken Clemençeau. Let me suggest soft-shell crabs for the girls, the chicken for you, Miss Hazel, soufflé potatoes béarnaise, shrimp and crab-meat rémoulade, and oysters en brochette to start? Sounds good?"

As was, and still is, the practice for locals, menus are rarely needed, and Nelson knew what they loved because the ladies all nodded.

"Very well, *mon cheri,* I'll be back in a flash with your drinks."

Suddenly, Vilma's face fell as she scanned the noisy room. She whispered quietly through a pleasant smile that never moved, "Oh my hell, here comes the aptly named Doris Strain, I am not in the mood, all she talks about is herself or something plain awful that befell her dearest and closest friend or money. Tacky witch. My word, she is intolerable. No wonder her husband turned homosexual. Oh yes, common knowledge. Audubon Park shelter number four. Please don't come over, oh please oh please . . . Oh, hello Doris dear," Vilma drawled, pure saccharin.

Doris was the sort of person who read reviews of theatre and books rather than experiencing them herself, then would quote the critics as if their words were her own. Although she was president of the Opera Guild, she knew nothing about opera and actually had to take No-Doz to remain awake during *Carmen,* no less. The only reason she vaguely recognized the melodies was because of reruns of *Gilligan's Island* that featured the classic Verdi score as the basis for a musical version of *Hamlet.*

"Hello, ladies, Miss Hazel, Miss Gayle, what brings y'all to the Quarter today?"

They all knew better than to answer, because before they could even start, she went on, "I am having lunch with some dear college sorority sisters from Jackson, and then we are going to have a good ol' time spending our husbands' money over by Holmes's for a start."

A telltale sign of class level in the Big Easy lay in whether one pronounced the name of the popular department store D. H. Holmes in the possessive. Doris continued, "I intend on wearing down the little letters on my New Orleans Shopper Card. Do y'all have one? It's a dream, I tell you, a modern miracle of a dream. They just put these letters on your plastic card . . ."

Moozie mentioned that they all had a New Orleans

Shopper Card, but it went unnoticed as Doris continued rambling. So Moozie just buttered the hot French bread before it cooled. She wasn't about to miss out on one of her favorites because of this overprivileged, underaccomplished twit.

"... G is for Godchaux's, K is for Kreeger's, MB is for Maison Blanche, and so on. And they just send the bill. Just like here, don't you just love having a house charge at restaurants? We have one at all the ones we love, it just makes it so much easier, not having to deal with dirty cash. I love just saying 'house charge,' it's so much more refined, like a country club. Gayle, we missed you at the Crippled Children's Hospital Guild meeting this morning, and both you girls don't forget the Protestant Home for Unwed Mothers tea on Thursday. I tell you, my darling hubby is a living doll, he really is, I don't know what I did to deserve such a sweetie, I honestly don't. I am a member of a bajillion organizations, president of two, vice president of one, and secretary of another, and he never complains about all the fundraisers and galas and all that jazz. Not a peep. I do declare he is an angel, an angel on earth. Did you all hear about Sue and Pierre? Separated. He was shacking up with something on the side just blocks from here."

Mother stared past Doris and muttered the word "Angel."

With this, Doris stopped flapping, pulled her head back, and squinted, saying "I beg your pardon, Gayle dear."

Vilma took her wounded sister's hand and gave it a gentle squeeze as if to revive her from this trance.

Mom smiled and tilted her head slightly, took a sip from her recently delivered drink, and sighed, calling forth ever so slightly Olivia de Havilland's Melanie. "Well, Doris, it must be just heaven, having an angel for a husband."

Moozie could stand no more. She'd never liked this woman, no one did. They all tolerated her, but that was about to come to an end. Besides, this was not how she intended to pass this particular luncheon. She said, "I don't know about you, but I always like a little devil in my men. Get my drift, honey?" She emphasized the word "devil," raising an eyebrow and buttoning the comment with a wink and a bite of celery.

This retort came as quite a shock to her daughters, but more to Doris, who feigned a giggle that ended as she snorted, "Oh, Miss Hazel, you are a card, and you must be dealt with."

Moozie's dander was up, way up, and luckily for all present, Miss Doris quickly spotted another victim across the chatty den whose lunch she saw fit to sour. And with a faux smile punctuated by insincere air kisses, she mercifully fled to a table of unsuspecting oversized-hat-wearing ladies who lunch.

"Well now, it is quite clear she has mastered one-half of the art of conversation," Moozie said as she buttered another hearty bite of bread, letting the crumbs fall to the white tablecloth, as is the custom at Galatoire's.

Vilma added, "See, somebody always has it worse than you. I mean, I wouldn't want to dance in her shoes, even if they do cost an arm and a leg—and that makeup!"

"There is a limit to what a single solitary eyelid can

bear," Moozie declared as they both giggled like school-girls.

"Oh, sister, come on, it's just a little cat-talk, and honestly, Mother, you were in rare form, two for two!"

Mom thought for a second, and shook her head softly. "You know, I never could gossip, I just don't like it, ever since I was a little girl and Reverend Storm gave that sermon where he talked about how gossip was like cutting open a down pillow on a windy day, and trying to take it back would be like getting all those feathers back in the casing—impossible, and just because of a few words. Well, I don't want them to talk about me that way, especially now, so how can I?"

"You know I was just trying to make you laugh, take your mind off things," Vilma defended.

"I know, and I love you for it, both of you. But that woman is hurting, and so am I, we just show it in different ways." She took a long sip of her Bloody Mary, then popped an anchovy olive in her mouth and continued, "Dr. Waters calls that compensating; some people go overboard in the opposite direction to avoid the truth. He says it's a manifestation of—"

Moozie interrupted, "Oh, for crying out loud!" Just as Nelson arrived with their meal, "And thank the Lord, Nelson, you got here just in time."

While Moozie was diverted by the appetizers, Vilma winked and shrugged to Mom as she had done since they were children, and Mom returned the gesture; it was their code, their mutual comment on their mother.

After the delicious meal and café brûlot dramatically

served flaming from a silver bowl with awe-inspiring ladle dexterity, the ladies made their way to Canal Street, to Adler's, for the true purpose of the mission.

Mom paused for a moment under the grand bronze clock that landmarked the classic nineteenth-century structure, but instantaneously her cohorts locked arms on either side and marched her through the heavy glass doors, up to the main jewelry counter, where Mr. Wally stood poised for the sale.

He smiled. "Always a pleasure, Mrs. Batt, ladies. How may I assist you today?"

Then the feeding frenzy began. Brilliant diamonds and creamy pearls can sometimes take one's mind off the everyday pains of life, at least for a few minutes. Some women have a weakness for shoes, some for designer clothes, some for furs. My mother's passion is jewelry; she simply adores it. Mr. Wally presented diamond clip earrings set in gold, composed of many pear-shaped, top-quality stones that fit the shape of her ear to perfection. "Those will do," she muttered. "To be honest, I've had my eye on these for a while." The suggestions and commentary came rapid-fire, so much that Mr. Wally didn't know whom to answer first, nor could he get a word in edgewise.

"Those are *heaven.*"

"You think so? They're not too much?"

"John will kill me."

"Just let him try."

"Oh, look at those, my stars, they are breathtaking, how many carats?"

This banter and flurry continued for what seemed like

an eternity for Mr. Wally, but it was really under an hour. In the end, the girls decided on the diamond and gold clips, because they could be worn during the day to a dressy luncheon. However, Moozie made it clear that she didn't care for the new jewel rules; diamonds were not for day-wear, despite what the Duchess of Windsor said. But they were all in agreement on the pearls, a double strand of opera-length with a diamond and gold clasp that complemented the earrings and allowed many options for wear.

Mom nodded. "Thank you, Wally, you have been a dear, I'll take it. Oh, and 'house charge' Pontchartrain Beach. Please make sure the bill goes to my husband's office."

"That'll get him," Moozie whispered.

When they arrived home, Mom's face lost all color as she saw my father's car in the garage. She started to sink, but when Moozie stopped, she quickly hopped out, thanking them for everything but explaining that she had to do this alone, no matter how difficult.

They blew kisses and lovingly told her she would be fine, to just stand her ground, and call as soon as possible. Carrying her handbag on one arm and the small shopping bag on the other, she approached the front door and, rather than ringing the bell, began the characteristic fruitless search for her keys, when Dad suddenly opened the door.

His face was drawn and his eyes glassy and bloodshot, but not from drinking. She stared into his eyes, eyes that she had loved since her junior year at Newcomb College. She stood at the threshold and looked at their home in a completely different light. She asked softly, "Where's Oralea?"

"I gave her the afternoon off."

"Where are the boys?"

"Riding bikes. I'm sorry. I am so sorry."

She stepped into the foyer, letting the door slowly close behind her, not saying a word.

"She means nothing to me, it was only once."

"Once was enough."

"I never meant to hurt you, you are the only woman I've ever loved, please forgive me."

Even though his words sounded clichéd and cinematic, his delivery was sincere. She knew this man, now she knew even more, maybe more than she wanted. She had heard of other men's affairs, and had thought it could never happen to her, but it had. But that was just it, it had, past tense, and it would not happen again. Somehow the words just came out. Although she had rehearsed a perfect rant in her head, the words were soft but crystal-clear and sharp as razors.

"I will be able to forgive you, one day. But I swear, John, if you dare do it to me again, you will regret the day you were born. Now, we will never speak of it again in this house."

"Never?" he asked hopefully, questioning his good fortune.

"Oh darling, we will discuss it, once every week, just not in this house. I called Dr. Waters and he has recommended a marriage counselor, so now we will have a standing appointment. And if you are a good boy, I may one day let you take me to lunch before it."

"All right." Dad sighed. He didn't like it, but it was fair. A few tense moments passed, then he noticed the Adler's bag.

"Honey, what's in the bag?"

"Just a few baubles to help ease my pain." She turned to face the gilded mirror above the console, opened the boxes, and slowly adorned herself with the new gems. "I hope you don't mind, I sent the bill to the beach."

"But Gayle, how am I going to explain that to Dad?"

She spoke to the reflection in the mirror. "I honestly don't know or really care, but somehow I have a feeling he'll understand, Johnny. Have you taken a good look at your mother's brooch collection? Look at the fire in those diamonds, five carats total."

"Okay, honey," he said, as a sad smile came across his face. He had loved giving her jewelry in the past, having helped design special rings for anniversaries or charms for her bracelet celebrating special occasions, but there was no joy in this.

Mom's eyes filled with tears as she gently removed the glittering ear clips, tilting her head left to right, as she softly said, "And they go back to Adler's tomorrow. Every sparkle of every diamond will just remind me of this, and I don't want to celebrate it, I want to bury it." She stared in the mirror a few moments longer, lifted her head, and announced, "Except the pearls, they don't sparkle, they luster!"

Fashion = Porn

MOM NEVER LET herself go entirely, but she'd developed a progressive lapse in fashion judgment that weighed heavily on my prepubescent brain. And ever since meeting Aunt Gretchen, I was inspired to transform her. Mom's hair was teased, coiffed, and varnished, and her makeup and nails were always polished and painted to perfection. She was at the height of 1960s style. Unfortunately it was the Year of Our Lord 1976. An entire decade had passed with unfortunately only a few very minor adjustments. Truth be told, I didn't want her to be embarrassed, but moreover, I didn't want to be embarrassed. Puberty and braces are quite enough, thank you. By junior high, I had become extremely clothes-conscious. I had to have the right Izod shirts and the right Wallaby shoes, conforming to the trends set by the Newman upperclassmen. At bedtime I would pick out my ensemble for the next school day before watching Johnny Carson on my tiny black-and-white Sony.

I extended this love of fashion and concern over appearance to my mother. I knew she shouldn't wear what the kids were wearing, nor should she dress as an identical twin of her mother, but at the same time I somehow knew there had to be a happy medium, a more progressive fashion-forward image for her. It was the age of the natural look, peasant flounced skirts with boots, wrap skirts, and macramé belts. I noticed these fashion trends from the high-end extreme of Aunt Gretchen to the varied looks on the street and in the department stores, and although Mom was in her early forties, her look had become that of a matron. She seemed sadly stuck in a time warp. Double-knit A-line dresses with matching jackets and handbags only Queen Elizabeth would consider. It was crystal clear that Mom was out of step, not herself, and needed a personal stylist, but who could it be?

Remodeling and updating my mom's look became my personal crusade. Rule number one, the very first commandment: never wear the same dress as your mother. And that rule applies to everyone. Other rules and ideas would come as my fashion education progressed. For example, I soon realized that frosted lipstick was definitely out.

Uncharacteristically, Mom eagerly embraced the chance to change. The self-help movement was sweeping the nation, and books like *I'm OK, You're OK, Jonathan Livingston Seagull,* and *The Sensuous Woman* were on the best-seller lists. Mom got swept away.

First she tackled her weight. Gloria Marshall lady's spa, where a multitude of machinery jiggled the fat away, was contacted and frequented. Soon there were exercise devices at home. One such engineering marvel resembled a chiropractic table where three separate Naugahyde-upholstered platforms would simultaneously gyrate in opposing directions. The other involved a large strap attached to an even larger vibrating apparatus worn around the waist or posterior, which virtually shimmied the excess pounds into oblivion. I think the latter was invented for men's viewing pleasure just as much as for ladies' fitness.

But that wasn't enough. Over the next several months, Mom ingested heaps of an amino acid and liquid protein supplement concoction and was injected weekly with a now illegal dietary substance, administered by a physician of questionable credentials in the far-off suburb of Kenner. Her figure and her long-lost body image eventually returned.

But hers wasn't the only metamorphosis that summer. I finally started to develop a caterpillar above my upper lip, as well as hair under my arms and "down there." My whole face started to change for the better. As a child, no matter the season, my complexion was bright white, with flushed cheeks, crowned by a moppish shock of thick jet-black locks that genetically fell straight into my eyes above a red-lipped, oversized mouth. I was a cross between a black Labrador retriever puppy, Jerry Lewis, and a clown. I thanked God that a new look was on its way, even if it did include a uni-brow. I constantly prayed that if I had to be hairy, please let me look like Mark Spitz or KC of KC and the Sunshine Band. The only problem was that my voice had not started to change yet, and it infuriated me when Mom's friends would call, and I'd be mistaken for the "lady of the house."

When I wasn't just hanging out watching TV, riding bikes, climbing trees, or making tapes with my childhood pal Chucky, I would covertly sneak away and pedal to the Lakefront neighborhood's overpriced drugstore, Krown Drugs, and "house charge" fashion magazines to "the Beach." I was sure to say, "They're for my mom."

And the gum-smacking checkout chick, with a hairstyle three years even more out of date than my mom's, would smile and coo in her perfect "Yat" accent. Derived from the phrase "where ya at," Yat is a colorful vernacular dialect of the Big Easy.

"Na ain't you a sweet lil dawlin' hawt you."

The Yat accent sometimes is reminiscent of Brooklynese, slowed down with a thick, lazy Southern drawl.

Nevertheless, I had my copies of *Vogue, Harper's Bazaar,* and the most European, *L'Officiel,* and the great work of fashion had begun. I pored for hours on end over the collections, fascinated by the different styles of the designers and the use of fabric, as well as the fantastic photography of masters like Avedon and Scavullo. There was something very provocative and sexy about the editorial photography and the dramatic scenarios on the glossy and addictive pages of these publications. A new, exciting, glamorous world, one that took me away from the sometimes difficult and awkward world of thirteen. Very soon I could identify an Oscar de la Renta even among a grouping of Yves Saint Laurent, Scassi evening gowns, and could tell the difference between Calvin and Anne Klein. They were not related, you know. Reading these magazines, I noticed all the great stores that advertised in them: Saks Fifth Avenue, I. Magnin, Bonwit Teller, Nieman Marcus, and Sakowitz. Assuming the selection of designer fashion was greater in these bigger cities, I called information, got the numbers, and then dialed long distance. When the operator answered, I asked, "With whom do I speak about receiving your fashion catalog in the mail?"

And inevitably the operator would respond, "Yes, ma'am, I'll connect you," or "Please hold, ma'am."

This time I didn't mind too much being mistaken for my mother; I was getting what I wanted and using what I had to get it! The fashion catalogs would come. I noted when the mailman dropped the post, which directly entered my father's home office, and slyly retrieved them. No one knew or ever complained about the unusually high phone bill, either.

I would rip out the pages of the fashion magazines and tape them on the refrigerator with my comments made in red marker: "This could work for you," or "Gaucho's, take a chance?" At first she was a little hesitant, but after the salesladies in practically all the designer and better-dresses departments commented, "Mrs. Batt, your son has excellent taste," or "I'm so impressed that a thirteen-year-old knows who Geoffrey Beene is," she was sold.

The clincher was a big supper dance for the International Amusement Park convention, which was to be held in New Orleans. It was a black-tie event, and Jay and I were included. Mom was so flustered with renting us tuxedos that she really didn't consider what she would wear. Her closet was amply filled with evening gowns that she wore to the carnival ball. When she told me what she was planning to wear, I was in shock.

"Mom, are you kidding? Dad's like some host for this big huge event and you are going to show up in a burgundy chiffon with a beaded top? It's April, for God's sake. You need an off-the-shoulder peasant blouse with a taffeta skirt, you know, like the Russian peasant thing Yves Saint Laurent is doing—only in spring colors."

There wasn't much time, but we headed to Canal Street and within minutes I picked out the perfect dress, and the saleslady confirmed my choice. At the dinner dance Mom received a multitude of compliments on her dress, especially from Dad. After they came back from dancing to "Tenderly" (their song), Mom came over and kissed my cheek and whispered, "Thank you, monkey, you have no idea how good I feel tonight."

ONE PARTICULARLY STEAMY July afternoon, on a jaunt to Krown Drugs, my eyes were drawn to the men's magazines. There, on the cover of *GQ*, was a Greek god. Next, a huge young Austrian bodybuilder on the cover of *Muscle & Fitness*. Jackpot! But I could not buy these; somehow I knew people would find it strange. The checkout charmer would surely catch on. "They're for my mom" just wouldn't cut it this time, but I was on fire, my knees shaking. I simply had to possess those magazines. I had to look more closely at those forms. I didn't have long to think about why I felt this way because something else was happening, something that had never happened before in public, and certainly never from gazing at a male cover model or an Austrian bodybuilder—full-blown wood.

I quickly grabbed the two magazines and shoved them down my pants. Thank God I had worn my brother's old oversized Lacoste shirt, as it helped to cover both my sins. With overwhelming guilt and near-exploding hormones, I walked awkwardly to the checkout counter. Miss Dawlin' smacked out, "Just a *Vogue*? Why dontcha getcha mama one of dem *Cosmos* for a change, huh?"

"Maybe next time, I'm in a hurry."

"Don't sweat it, baby—sign here."

And I was the Tasmanian Devil on my ten-speed, pedaling like mad to get to my room as quickly as my skinny legs would take me. Up the concrete sidewalk, onto the oil-stained brick driveway, into the garage, bike slung to the floor like an abused Apache dancer. Just then I was stopped by the ever-present Oralea.

"Chile, you straighten up that bike, I swear, don't you think I've got better things to do than pick up after you boys, I'm telling your mama that I ain't touching your room no more, it's plain disgusting. And why are you holding your stomach? You don't feel well? Let me go get the thermometer."

"No, no . . . sorry, I'm fine, really . . . I just have to . . . go to the bathroom. This is for Mom."

With that, I plopped down the *Vogue* on the Formica countertop, ran through the den, flew up the stairs into my room, locked the doors, and searched for a place to hide my new treasure.

As the weeks passed and the beastly hot days of summer were coming to an end, my paternal grandparents, Mom-ee and Da-Dee, invited the whole family, as they often did, to the Sazerac Restaurant at the Fairmont Hotel, which locals, my family included, defiantly referred to as the Roosevelt, for that's what it had been called for decades prior. It was an old grand hotel and a sight to behold at Christmas, but its crowning glory, besides the famed Blue Room, where, years before, I'd seen Carol Channing in a life-altering cabaret show, was the famed Sazerac. It was one of my favorite restaurants in the city because of the sheer theatricality of the décor. Deep red velvet bunting and draperies adorned the walls, and tremendous, opulent floral creations graced the tops of pillars throughout the space.

But the pièce de la résistance was the individual ice-sculpted swan used to serve the glacé that was served to cleanse the palate before the entrée. It was presented to the patrons upon a velvet stand containing a disguised battery-operated light that illuminated the swan from underneath, creating a magical vision. I loved to order the most adventurous appetizers and entrée to get a rise out of Da-Dee. At ten years old I ordered escargot because I saw Lucy do it on her Parisian trip on *I Love Lucy*. Da-Dee chided, "Son, do you even know what that is? Have you ever tried it?"

I replied, "Yes, Da-Dee, it's snails, but I want to try it

and use the cool clamp thingy that's supposed to hold the shell and not your nose."

He loved it that I would try any kind of cuisine; he had no tolerance for people who eschewed anything without at least experiencing it first. Because of his influence, I added to my favorites not just escargot, but Oysters Rockefeller and Bienville, fois gras, and my favorite, sweetbreads. He also loved and encouraged my theatricality, and every time we passed the Blue Room to dine at the Sazerac, he would ask me to do my Carol Channing imitation, which tickled Da-Dee but worried my father.

After the culinary feast, we all made our way to the parking garage directly across the street, passing a newsstand. Da-Dee gave me a few dollars and said, "Bryan, pop in there, son, and get Da-Dee a copy of the *Wall Street Journal,* and keep the change."

So I did. The crew ambled to retrieve their respective cars, the men discussing city politics and the women admiring Mom-ee's latest jewelry acquisition.

The ramshackle kiosk was filled with every kind of newspaper and periodical, and smelled of menthol cigarettes. As I walked toward the rear, I noticed fashion magazines I'd never seen before, some in French and Italian. Who knew such treasures could be found in such a dismal hole? My eyes kept scanning the rows and rows until they came across the male-for-male porn section. *Honcho, Blue Boy*—names I'd never seen before or even understood. I was flushed and shaking now. Then my retina literally burned as I saw images beyond my wildest imagination.

Preoccupied, I jumped when the crusty shopkeeper muttered, "Whatchoo want, son?"

I stuttered, "A *Wall Street Journal,* please."

The toothless man forcefully presented the paper with his nicotine-stained hands. His nails were filthy, and on his wrinkled forearm was a distorted tattoo that, due to his age and lack of sunscreen or hygiene, made the figure indecipherable. He gave me the change, and I hoped our hands would not touch. I put a quarter in the tip tray and quickly began my exit as he said, "You sure you don't want anything else?"

"No thank you," I said nervously, quickening my gait, never glancing back.

For the next two days the only thought on my mind was those magazines at the newsstand next to the Fairmont, rather the Roosevelt. It wasn't as if I could charge them to the Beach or pilfer them under my shirt. Mr. Crusty would certainly notice. What randy images lived on those pages? The cover models alone were enough, but if what lurked inside was the male version of my father's *Playboy* collection, I had to see. I simply had to.

I tried to divert these pangs by poring over the collection of catalogs, deciding what Mother should purchase for her fall wardrobe. Then—inspiration on page seventeen of Neiman's. The model in the earth-tone-patterned Diane von Furstenberg wrap dress told me exactly what to do to get those magazines. It was as if she spoke from the page, "Make the call, make the call," with her lips pursed and pouty.

Checking to see if the coast was clear and that neither

Jay nor Oralea was in sight, I quickly dialed information
on the Mickey Mouse phone in the upstairs playroom
and asked the operator for the telephone number of Bon
Marché News on Baronne Street, the one next to the Roosevelt. I nervously dialed the extension, and when Mr.
Crusty answered, I more than imitated Mother's voice:

"Hello. Is this the Bon Marché News, the one next to
the Roosevelt? . . . Yes, well, I honestly cannot believe I
am making this call, but anyhoo, my niece is getting married shortly, and her bridal party and sisters are actually
having one of those bachelorette parties. To tell you the
truth, I'd never heard of such a thing until I watched it
on *Donahue*. They got a crazy notion to put me in charge
of getting some gag-like things, like the bachelors do, so
I asked like what, and they thought it would be a hoot
and a half if I got . . . you know . . . dirty magazines, you
know . . . as a joke. I Sewanee, in my day we never did
such a thing. I think they're just trying to make me blush,
their 'square aunt' . . . well, we'll just show them, won't
we?"

It was a masterful channeling of her voice and manner,
if I do say so. Continuing the charade, I asked Mr. Crusty
to please put aside *Playgirl, Honcho, Blueboy,* and a French
Vogue magazine, but be sure to wrap them up well, and
mark them "do not open," as "she" was too embarrassed
to come fetch them herself, so she was sending her young
son as courier.

"What name shall I hold them under, ma'am?" he
asked.

"Well, uh . . . Bouvier, thank you," I replied.

The next morning, after barely finishing my frosted blueberry Pop-Tart, I announced that I was off to play and would not be home for lunch. Instead, I raced via the public service bus to the newsstand to pick up my prize.

Upon arrival, I looked at *Mad* magazine and *Sports Illustrated* until the store was devoid of other patrons, then I approached Mr. Crusty, and gave what I thought to be a deeply genuine and nuanced performance.

"Excuse me, sir, my mom sent me to pick some package up for her. She didn't say what it was. The name is, uh, Bouvier."

Mr. Crusty grinned, showing his lack of teeth, as he handed over the brown-paper-wrapped bundle. My hands trembled as I accepted it, fumbling for the money to pay him. And when he gave me the change, he looked me directly in the eyes and winked. "I hope these are enjoyed."

His hand touched mine for a second longer than it should have, and I turned and ran out of the store. Behind me I could hear his raspy, sinister laugh, and nearly was sick.

Then I headed straight for Lake Vista, and the levees of Lake Pontchartrain. I loved playing games on the vast promenades and climbing the endless number of trees in the park. But there would be no tree-climbing or game-playing today, just covert reading of fashion and porn, one fraught with beauty and couture, the other with sex and guilt—so much guilt that within days I had burned the magazines and flushed the remains down the toilet, only to cause severe plumbing issues that were never traced to me. It would be many years before mine eyes would see that glory again.

THERE HAD BEEN some changes that summer. Mom was no longer on the road to dowagerville, but had become a triumphant butterfly that I had helped to emerge from her style-lapsed cocoon. I too had undergone a transformation, physically becoming a man. Although I had instinctively sought to visit a world so foreign to me, fear caused a retreat to the world I thought I should live in, the one I was raised to live in, the only one I knew.

Big Red Riding Hood

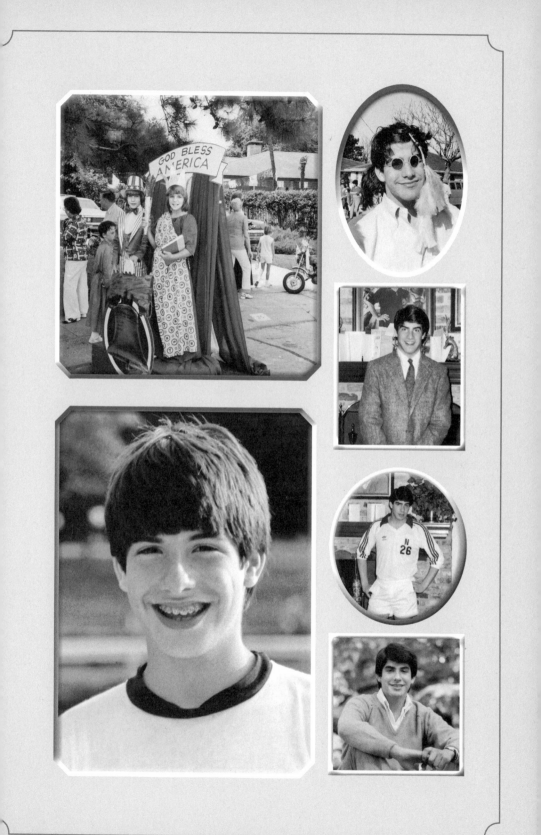

IN THE LATE SEVENTIES, probably the summer after seventh grade, while Mom and Dad were "working it out," Jay and I started "brothers therapy" so we wouldn't fight so much. Over the years, the sibling rivalry between us had grown alarmingly, and our antics had escalated to a point where warnings that had once scared us, like "Wait till your father comes home," or "I'm calling your father at the office," now didn't cause the slightest ebb in our misbehavior. And therapy really wasn't much help, either. One night Jay did something to provoke me, as he often did, and I threw a fork at him, which lodged in his thigh. That loss of temper and violent act cost me my pride and joy, my Fourth of July Parade.

My theatricality had continued to express itself in many forms, and a few years earlier I'd asked Mom to help me organize a patriotic, float-filled show-stopper of a Fourth of July Parade for our neighborhood. Mom jumped in with both feet, enlisting the support of neighbors and school friends as well as Jay's Little League team and Boy Scout troop. She contacted the press, marching bands, and church groups to participate, while I drew maps of the proposed route.

The first year's offering was modest in comparison to what the pageant became or could become in my loftiest of dreams. There were decorated wagons, convertible cars, and borrowed grocery carts. My buddy Chucky drove his go-cart with American flags flying; my friend Lee Adler dressed as an American eagle; Jay wore an Uncle Sam mask and didn't have an asthma attack. Of course I was the fife player of the iconic fife-and-drum corps, along with my cousin Kevin and school friend Dene carrying the flag and playing the drum.

The next year was even bigger and better. For Christmas I had asked for floats, which I am sure slightly startled my father; however, he did have five low-to-the-ground, rope-pulled, sturdy plywood-and-two-by-four structures built for me. (This holiday request was only to be surpassed a few years later when my love of antique furniture blossomed, and I asked for an eighteenth-century Chippendale secretary.) The theme was Great Americans, and I was to be George Washington. I researched eighteenth-century costume and drew an exact replica of General Washington's Revolutionary uniform as he crossed the Delaware. However, Mom and Moozie thought that the pink satin Spring Fiesta costume would suffice, just add a white periwig, and voilà! I was a bit frustrated as a few years had passed since that fateful spring night, and the pants were tight and short, so Miss Inez cut them below the knee and created more period-appropriate knickers. White knee socks were added, along with brass buckles on my shoes. All in all, it was all right, but I seriously doubt that General Washington ever wore a pale pink satin ensemble with a rose velvet cape, but I'm sure his Martha didn't sport a mod floral maxi-dress either.

When I formally presented the list of prospective Great Americans to grace the floats, Dad had some specific ideas. He thought it could be great to have categories like Great Inventors, so that float could have Henry Ford, Thomas Alva Edison, and Benjamin Franklin. A float dedicated to Great American Sportsmen could host Saints quarterback Archie Manning, Jim Thorpe, and more. This idea was a gold mine, and I was eager to start modifying my float sketches and casting the great Americans. I wasn't too pleased that Dad had pretty much insisted we have President and Pat Nixon represented on the presidents' float. However, in my float design the antiwar peace symbol was most prevalent. The family got roped into the act as well. Aunt Marilyn and Aunt Norma designed hundreds of red, white, and blue star-spangled decorations and helped hammer together several floats. In the an un-air-conditioned warehouse on the back lot of Pontchartrain Beach, Moozie and Mom covered the floats with red, white, and blue bunting, plastic fringe, and crepe paper. The parade was a big hit with the neighborhood, and beyond. The local ABC affiliate interviewed me for the nightly news, and I was awarded the key to the city.

All year I had been planning how to make this year's parade, our third, even better. My school notebooks were filled with float and costume designs celebrating this year's theme: Great Moments in American History. The floats would be grander than ever before, with stirring titles such as "The Pilgrims Land on Plymouth Rock," "The Signing of the Declaration of Independence," "The Civil War," and "Man Walks on Moon!" I was even trying to figure out ways to have automation so that the papier-mâché figures would move like in the big Mardi Gras parades. I would often ask the manager at the Piggly Wiggly or the Winn-Dixie grocery stores if I could have the battery-operated mechanism that was used in several moving advertising displays. If only I had known about hot glue, my life would have taken a completely different path.

My goals were high, and my dreams for the parade even higher. I knew my destiny and it all had to do with spectacle. But now, with one flick of my wrist, my parade, my glory, was history.

I was sent to sleep-away camp, and at first I loved the idea. We shopped for supplies and packed everything in a big trunk like I'd seen in the movies. Mine of course had to be decorated with bumper stickers and my special touch, my name spelled out in hand-painted bubble letters. While most of my friends went to camps on the Gulf Coast or even as far as North Carolina, my parents saw fit to ship this innocent to Camp Chippewa in Bemidji, Minnesota. Yes, Minnesota. I had heard of the state of many lakes before, but had never realized how far away it actually was. Later I wondered, *Just how far away did they need me?* Granted, I was a bit much at this age, a whirling dervish, a Tasmanian Devil of sorts, but Minnesota? The first night at camp, a terrifying feeling came over me and did not leave until Mom came to retrieve me on the very last day. At rustic Camp Chippewa I suffered the worst case of homesickness in sleep-away-camp history, constantly begging to talk to my parents and to go home. Instead of acquiescing, Mom thought it best for me to stick it out and encouraged me to participate in all of the camp activities. Giving up or giving in was not an option.

Sadly, I was still pathetic at sports. I tried to play basketball in seventh and eighth grades, but was embarrassingly horrific. I redefined the term "scrub," and would only get to play in a game if our team was winning like crazy or losing by an unbeatable amount. I would pray not to be put in the game, and still would rather watch the cheerleaders. There was one lad worse than me on the team, and he actually shot at the wrong goal and made two points for the opposition. He is now a gynecologist. So my only solace at camp was to sail. I learned to master the Sunfish sailboat quite easily, and taking that small slip of a boat out on Cass Lake filled me with a sense of freedom and accomplishment that I had never felt before. After a while I did open up, made a few friends, and enjoyed the experience a tiny bit more—canoe trips and sleeping in tents under the starry northern skies was so new—but I desperately longed for home, for my friends and my parade. To my surprise, my cabin mates thought I was funny. They laughed at my Carol Burnett imitations and acerbic commentary, but when I picked flowers and arranged them in a canteen on the cabin table for Sunday inspection, which won us a trip to the ice cream parlor, I became an official smartass.

Jay was also sent away that summer, to Menlo Park, California, for summer school. Our small unit had been strewn to the far corners of the map, Family Deconstruction 101. It was the first time we had ever really been separated, and when we returned home things were different; we didn't fight as much, but other storms were stirring.

BACK AT HOME, my father's drinking had reached its pinnacle and, as predicted, he suffered a massive heart attack. The physicians at Oschner Hospital noted that they had never seen such an enlarged heart. That's my family. If we are going to do it, it's going to be big.

My brother and I were pretty spoiled. Mom would later quip in her defense, "I may have spoiled you boys rotten, but you better never act like it." Confronted with her husband's bleak diagnosis, Mom realized that her children had lived a sheltered and privileged life with no chores or responsibilities. *What if John dies?* she thought. *What will we do?* She decided that Jay and I would now pull our weight, and although there was now a staff of two, Oralea and Howard (who did the heavier labor), from now on we would make our own beds every morning, and hers and Dad's on the weekends, set the table, clear the table, alternate doing the dishes, and weed the garden (most everyone we knew was still a bit apprehensive about allowing me to operate potentially limb-severing machinery). But the killer was that because of our lack of aiming skills, my brother and I would alternate weekends cleaning the toilets.

Such a big change, I thought—back from summer camp and descending from Little Lord Fauntleroy to Oliver Twist within weeks. But it was one of the wisest decisions she ever made. Many other changes were forthcoming. Dad had to take daily naps and eat healthy, salt-free meals and fresh vegetables. Quiet was enforced and a new menu was set, and there was little or no deviation from it. At first it was quite an adjustment, but she did not back down; a decision had been made unlike any before, and there would be no dissension. Dad would awaken bright and early with us now, no longer hungover in bed as we left for school. In fact he took to making us elaborate breakfasts, big stuffed omelettes and sectioned navel oranges, daily. Jay and I would get our fix of our favorite foods like traditional New Orleans red beans and rice, po'boys, and anything fried from the Newman cafeteria, but not at home. During his recovery, Dad spent days upon days designing a house he would build on the plot of land on Pratt Drive. Mom sat us both down and, with a combination of stoic strength and compassion, told us the truth about our father's diagnosis.

"Boys—no, you are not boys anymore, although you'll always be my sweet boys, you are young men." She took a deep breath and looked upward as she inhaled, lifting her head higher as if gathering strength from above. "Your father is very ill, and we have to do everything in our power to make this home a quiet and calm place for him to heal. You now have your chores and responsibilities. I am so serious about this. There will be no more fighting between you. If you two have a problem, you know to talk it out. I will not make idle threats. If you can't abide by these wishes, then we will have to look at boarding schools. I have all the faith in the world in you young gentlemen, and I know you will make your father and me very proud."

Mom continued to work on herself as well, embracing openness, self-discovery, and self-modification like a house afire. Her bedside table, desk, and kitchen table were covered with more and more self-help paperbacks and meditation tapes, as well as books from Al-Anon. No one wanted to believe my father was an alcoholic, especially us, but Mother never was one for denial or pretense. The cold, hard truth was that my father was killing himself with drink, and although powerless over this insidious disease, she was not allowing it to take her husband or her family or herself down without a fight. Through Al-Anon meetings she learned about the nature of this illness and imparted that knowledge to us boys. No matter what the drinker said, none of it was our fault. People drink because they drink. We cannot change others, only ourselves.

WITHIN A YEAR Dad was better and somewhat sober, but he never would be considered healthy again, while Mom was radiant and thriving as never before. Taking better care of herself than she had in years, she glowed with health and had reduced to a size eight, almost the same as when she wed. Within just a few short years she had completely reinvented herself, or, better yet, found herself, the true Gayle Batt, and there would be no turning back now. She blossomed in many other ways, too, taking on chairmanships and board positions with many arts and charitable organizations. She was becoming her own woman, her own creation. Still elegant, soft, and feminine, she was at the same time strong, determined, and courageous.

That same stripe of strength, determination, and courage would serve me well in high school and beyond. By freshman year, I tried to conform and be a typical Uptown New Orleans teen in my manner of preppy dress and my aloofish air, because after some teasing and name-calling I realized that the "artistic" kids were not accepted that well and were not hanging out with the cool kids. The desire to be popular and accepted by the cool kids outweighed my theatrical inclinations. I asked my cool friend and new neighbor Bjorn what I could do to be more cool. He said that sometimes I walked funny, and got too excited about uncool stuff. So I practiced walking in a more manly way, resisted performing the cheers along with the cheerleaders at all sports events, and, worst of all, I did not audition for any school plays or musicals. However, such rivers run very deep and could not be suppressed.

The touring company of the Broadway mega-hit *A Chorus Line* was coming to the Theater for the Performing Arts, and as Mom was always trying to get us to the theatre or the opera or the symphony or the ballet, I agreed enthusiastically to attend. After seeing that performance, three words then described my life: *never the same*. It was a revelation, and although I was very uncomfortable with some of the gay characters, as I still was very confused and extremely closed about my own tendencies, the entire evening was magic. It was a special magic that has stayed with me through the years, which I feel still today when I see or, better yet, am in a great show. It would not be until my junior year when Kitty Greenberg, Newman's head drama teacher and director, cornered me in the hall and pointedly and hypnotically said, "You, Bryan Batt, when are you going to audition for my play? You know you want to. I saw your Rudolph. You can't hide forever, mister, come to the cabaret!" After that I was a goner— but back to freshman year:

That same week I had somehow managed to pass the Louisiana driver's test. I was so proud to receive my driver's license, though it was not a monumental feat, given the horrific drivers we endure in the Big Easy, because it meant that now I could chauffeur Mom to glamorous events. Because of Dad's ill health, his social activity was restricted. Also, he loathed wearing a tuxedo or, even worse, tails, so the opera and carnival balls were fortunately scratched from his dance card. While Mom would get ready, dressing to the nines in gowns that I had hand-selected (like an elegant champagne Calvin Klein draped charmeuse silk), or that she found which had my stamp of approval, Dad would sit in his huge leather reclining wing chair in the handmade nightshirts Mom-ee made and watch the tube, including reruns of the original *Bob Newhart Show,* while eating an ice cream parfait, which eased the recovering drinker's craving for sugar.

On those evening trips with Mom, we would sing along to the eight-track tape of *A Chorus Line* over and over again in her big chocolate brown Cadillac. And even when we reached the song "Dance ten, looks three," we sang even louder, laughing at the lyrics "tits and ass." Eight-track tapes used to sometimes click over to the next track mid-song, and it always bothered me that it did so at the climax of Morales' "Nothing." In the song, Morales was in an acting class taught by Mr. Carp, a limited teacher. She was singing of how she was told to act like an ice cream cone and she tried to melt—when she had the realization that the class was nothing, and the teacher was nothing. Click.

"Bryanny boy, would you like to go to New York and see some shows on Broadway?" she asked one night out of the blue.

"Does a bear do it in the woods?" I responded.

"You boys with your crazy talk I am assuming that is a yes."

"Yeah, Mom, it's a definite yes."

The planning of the great trip began. My friends at school tolerated my excitement about going to New York and my giddiness about seeing my first Broadway show. Of course I tried to be cool and play it down by saying my mother and grandmother were making me go to New York, and I'd have to endure shows, shopping, and museums, but inside I was bursting with anticipation. Mom made reservations at the Plaza and contacted a broker for tickets to a few shows that friends had recommended. It was years since she had been to Manhattan. Owing to Dad's ongoing heart problems, their once-extensive life of travel had been severely curtailed.

"Coach, when I was a little girl, Moozie used to take me every year to New York for the Dance Masters of America convention, and we would see oodles of Broadway shows," Mom explained. "The original *Gypsy, My Fair Lady,* oh, just oodles. When I was your age, maybe a teensy bit younger, I was star-struck by Ingrid Bergman, and I had to see her in *Joan of Lorraine.* The play was sold out, but your Moozie and I went to the box office and somehow we had absolutely fabulous seats. Well, it was summertime and there was a heat wave. It was beastly hot and I had on a beautiful white eyelet dress with starched petticoats, just a dream of a dress. Anyhow, I was famished when we arrived at the theatre, so your grandmother bought me a big chocolate bar from the concession stand. Honey, when the lights went out and the play started, I was mesmerized, and Ingrid Bergman is a fabulous actress, you know. I didn't even realize how hot it was in the theatre, but by intermission the chocolate bar had melted all over my dress and gloves. It was a mess, but I didn't care. I just tossed the gloves in my handbag, and never let that purse move an inch from covering the stain. But I will never forget the magic of that performance."

She handed me a *New York* magazine and said, "Now, in the theatre section you will see listings of all the shows we already have tickets to: *Annie, Dancin',* and *Ain't Mis-*

behavin', plus another play, but the title has slipped my mind. If there is something that you want to see, let me know and I will call the broker to get tickets. I want this to be a special trip, little man."

I kissed her on the cheek and quickly took the magazine to my room. Salivating over the fashion ads for all the best stores, wondering where we would go and what we would see, I finally reached the Broadway listings. There it was, the show I was destined to see, *Gilda Radner Live from the Winter Garden*. It was the early years of *Saturday Night Live*, and although everyone was imitating Chevy Chase, John Belushi, and Dan Aykroyd, I was drawn to the wacky brilliance of Gilda.

"Mom!" I screamed from the top of the stairs, "I found the show!" Bounding down into the den with the magazine in hand, I announced, "It's got to be *Gilda Radner Live from the Winter Garden*."

"Okay, pet, I'll call right now."

The show was a limited summer engagement and had been sold out for months, and seats were impossible to get, which was not sitting well with Gayle Batt. Never one to give up, she assured me that she would do everything to procure seats.

Finally our travel day arrived. As usual, Mom was running late primping and last-minute packing, so there was some tension in the air as we got ready to go to the airport for our flight. People still dressed to fly in those days. I wore a tie. Eventually every bag was loaded in the massive trunk of the silver blue Fleetwood, and thanks to

Dad's lead-footed driving, we made it to Moisant Airport just in time to board the Eastern Airlines nonstop evening flight to New York's LaGuardia Airport.

"Jesus Christ, Gayle," he sighed, "y'all have enough luggage for a grand European tour. You're just going for a few days."

She smiled as she retorted, "Johnny, the Lord's name, and it's four days but six shows."

He caught my eye in the rearview mirror and said, "Son, whenever your grandfather would travel, he'd say, 'Before you leave, make sure you've got your spectacles, testicles, wallet, and watch.'"

I chuckled, but of course Mom and Moozie each just raised an eyebrow. As we all hurried down the terminal to board the plane, Dad slipped me some cash and said to treat the "ladies" to a drink on the plane and to pay for all the cabs. Giving me a big hug, he told me to watch out for them and keep my eyes peeled, New York was a dangerous city. In a flash we were seated and airborne, holding hands as the plane rose over the orange and pink sunset-lit swamps and the dark waters of Lake Pontchartrain.

As instructed, I treated my ladies to their cocktails, receiving adoration for my chivalry from the stewardess, and although we chatted about what we would see and Moozie and Mom recalled their many wonderful trips to the city, the flight seemed to take forever. I must have dozed off for a short while, only to be awakened by Mother tapping my knee softly, saying calmly but with a thrill in her voice, "Son, look at the lights."

It was a clear summer's night, and the lights of New

York glistened and twinkled more than the stars in the heavens, but it was just the beginning of the sparkle and wonder I felt. On the cab ride to the Plaza, Mom had the taxi driver pass Bloomingdale's and designer boutiques and other famous locales, so that we would arrive at the Plaza's front steps via glamorous Fifth Avenue. We had two adjoining rooms on the fourteenth floor, with breathtaking views of Central Park and the towers of the Manhattan skyline. I looked over at Mom, and she smiled. "Do you love it?" she asked.

And without hesitation I answered, "One day I'll live here, I've got to be here."

Her classic smile grew, maybe because there was yet another joy we could both share, or, more likely, that I was gently releasing the apron strings I had tied so tightly. After Camp Chippewa, the odds that I would ever stray from the side of Gayle Batt's hoop skirt were slim, but all it took was a trip to the Big Apple and a Broadway show to snip them.

At 10:00 a.m. sharp, we had a room-service breakfast and then we went to the Winter Garden Theater, where we were first in line at the ticket window. The marble lobby was much smaller than I'd imagined it would be, and I was taken by the photos of Gilda and Father Guido Sarducci on the walls. The blind rose on the advance ticket sales window, signaling Mom to make her move.

"Hello, we would like three seats for tonight's performance, please."

"Sorry, ma'am, the run is sold out."

Turning up the syrup factor on her Southern accent,

she lilted, "Oh, dear sir, this is my son's very first trip to New York and his little heart is set on seeing Miss Gilda Radner. Is there anything you can do? There must be some seats somewhere."

"Ma'am, it's sold out."

"But we flew all the way from New Orleans just to see this show, and if we don't, his little ol' heart will just break. I remember my first show, *Joan of Lorraine* . . .""

As she went on and on, telling the story in her most charming way, batting her lashes, I noticed him softening until finally he said, "All right, all right. Let me see what I can do."

He stepped away from the window back into the office, while Mom turned to me smiling and crossing both sets of fingers.

The man returned. "Ma'am, this is your lucky day. I can give you three in the house left box."

"Give? Oh, you sweet thing, I insist on paying for them."

They both shared a laugh, and she paid for the seats and we were off to meet Moozie at Saks for a day of shopping. Mom never gave up, no matter what. Even if the answer was no, she would just keep on trying. Nothing was ever impossible, she'd say; just try a different approach. She could and still can get whiskey from a rock, as Oralea once noted.

The rhythm and energy of the streets flowed through me like electricity. I'd never felt anything like it before. Not having had sex yet, New York was the closest thing. Saks was a revelation, with floor after floor of designers' collections. Even the best stores back home were small, with only a few pieces from the runway shows, and here was the whole enchilada—every designer I had ever heard of was represented in a big splashy way. Amid the frenzy, and drunk with retail, we realized it was nearing five-thirty and the curtain was at eight, so we rushed to get a taxi, a futile attempt at that hour on Fifth Avenue. So we hoofed it back to the hotel to the strains of Moozie's complaints about her knees and feet and why didn't we think ahead, but I was high on New York, and was loving every rushed, wonderful moment.

We arrived at the Plaza starving and exhausted. Moozie suggested that we order a light snack and get dinner after the show, so that's what we did. She put her feet up for a moment, and then the flurry of the Southern belles preparing for a big night in the big city began. I showered and shaved the caterpillar over my lip, and hopelessly tried to make the part stay in my thick mane. I dressed in a pair of bright red sailcloth summer pants, a white button-down oxford shirt, and a red plaid madras tie and a navy blazer; I looked like a preppy nightmare. Uncharacteristically, Mom emerged first into my room with a waft of Trigère perfume she'd acquired earlier in the day at Bergdorf's.

"Darlin', would you zip me, please?" which I did. "Now what about jewelry?"

I quickly answered with transparent insincerity, "Mom, really, whatever you want, it doesn't matter to me. Okay, triple-strand pearls, South Sea pearl and gold clips and brooch . . . "

"Thanks, pet. Mother, are you almost ready? Bryanny

boy, why don't you go downstairs and get in the queue—
that's what they call it up here, it's not a line, it's a queue—
for a taxi. As I recall, it's murder getting a cab this time of
night."

"Yes, but please hurry, I don't want to be late."

She winked as she handed me the tickets. "Yes sir."

I was next in line—sorry, the queue—when the two
magnolias appeared at the top of the red-carpeted stairway of the Plaza. They stood out from the crowd, but in
a good way, a softer way. I couldn't believe that Moozie
was wearing white kid gloves.

The taxi whisked us to the corner of 50th Street and
Broadway under the great marquee with its enormous pic-
tures of Gilda with her frizzy wild hair. Moozie took one
look at the photos and said, "Oh God, I hope we are not
seeing this show. That child is a mess. Does she even own
a comb? Who in heaven would let themselves be photo-
graphed looking like something the cat dragged in, much
less place it on the marquee of a Broadway theater?"

Mom tried to intervene by softly whispering, "Now,
Mother . . ."

But the cabdriver beat her to it. "I hear ya, lady, I hear
ya," he said.

The houselights were already blinking when we arrived, and we were guided to our seats by the lace-collared
usherette. We passed through the velvet curtains and up a
set of stairs to the box seats. There were three freestanding
chairs covered in the same velvet as the curtains; the usherette handed us our *Playbills,* and told us to enjoy the
show before she closed the curtains behind her. Mom in-

sisted that I push my seat to the front, and she and Moozie would sit behind. Meanwhile, Moozie went on about how she remembered seeing Al Jolson at this very theater, and Mom mentioned that they also saw *West Side Story* here as well, to which Moozie replied, "Oh, the dancing was just fantastic in that show, but talk about sad sad sad, I thought I'd cry my eyes out, remember we had to go to the Astor roof for a drink to shake it off?"

Mom thought for a second, "No, Mother, I believe that was *Death of a Salesman*."

"You are right, how could I forget that giddy little romp! I don't know why people write such depressing things. When I go to the theatre or movies, I want to be entertained and see beauty, not tragedy or, worse, vulgar language. Why can't people say what they have to say nicely?"

"Moozie, everyone's taste is different," I chimed in.

Mom added, smiling coyly, "That's right, Miss Hazel, something for everyone."

"Well, that's all fine and dandy, just give me something pretty, that's all I ask for, and please don't make me think too much, let me just sit back and be entertained."

Just then the lights dimmed and the orchestra started to play. A rush of excitement shook me as I felt Mom's hand gently patting my shoulder. The short overture stopped abruptly, a white-hot spotlight hit the curtain center stage, and out came Gilda to thunderous applause, wearing pink overalls and sporting frizzy pigtails. She began to sing a simple, juvenile-sounding little ditty, about talking dirty to barnyard animals:

"Fuck you, Mr. Bunny, eat shit, Mr. Bear,
If they don't love it, they can shove it, frankly I
don't care. Oh . . ."

At this very moment there was crazed laughter and
more applause, but I feared that Moozie was going to grab
me by the scruff of my neck with her gloved hand, drag
me down the stairs, and put me in a cab home to New Orleans. Good-bye, city life. With great trepidation, I slowly
turned my head to see both Mom and Moozie laughing so
much that they were dabbing their eyes with their han-
kies. Safe. And so Gilda continued talking dirty to the
animals, from the birds in the trees to snakes in the grass,
and warning how never, ever to tell an alligator to bite her
snatch!

And thus my Broadway musical theatre cherry was officially popped.

The rest of the show consisted of highlights of her great
SNL characters like Emily Latella and Rosanne Rosanna-
danna. We all stood for the ovation, and laughed nonstop
in the cab back to the Plaza.

Years later, when Moozie was nearly bedridden and
her memory was failing, she often asked me how that cute
girl we saw in New York was doing. I never had the heart
to tell her she had died so young.

Spent from the day of endless shopping and side-
splitting laughter, we stumbled into our rooms and simultaneously realized we were starving. Mom suggested
we call the famous Carnegie Deli and order some delicious pastrami or corned-beef sandwiches. This brilliant

idea was unanimously and instantly approved. She called and ordered, then turned to me, tilted her head, and said, "Bryanny, would you be a heart and walk over and pick up the sandwiches? The gentleman—well, I really shouldn't call him that, judging how short he was with me on the phone—well, pet, they are short a delivery boy, so honey, would you mind?"

Moozie said sternly, "Gayle, are you going to let that boy out on the streets of New York at this hour? Have you lost your mind?"

Mom replied confidently, "Mother, he is a young man. He is fifteen years old. Besides, it's just around the corner on Seventh Avenue. He'll be fine, won't you, pumpkin-eater boy?"

"Mom, if I'm a young man, then don't you think 'pumpkin-eater boy' can be retired? Moozie, I'll be fine. I'll put on a tough New York City face. See!"

I made the face that I'd been practicing in the mirror, like the glower of the *GQ* models I admired.

"Oh, tomato, that will ward off the robbers," Moozie laughed.

Mom handed me the money from her handbag, and I was off. I crossed the street in order to catch another glimpse of the fabulous window display at Bergdorf's. The streets were considerably quieter and less manic than during the daylight hours. As I progressed west on 57th Street to Seventh Avenue, the people on the street seemed to change a bit. This was the New York City of the late seventies, and two blocks west of Fifth Avenue was not what it is today. With each block I walked, I became more and more apprehensive under the stares of the citizens of the night. The moody model-man glower was not really working.

At last I crossed the avenue and arrived at the Carnegie Deli, paid for the order, and started back to the Plaza, this time on the west side of Seventh. As I walked, taking big steps and increasing my pace, I noticed three tall figures coming toward me, and suddenly a great blanket of fear passed over me. I couldn't turn and run, and there was nowhere to go but forward, but as they came toward me I realized they were women in extremely high-heeled platform shoes. As we passed, I tried like hell not to make eye contact, but somehow I was unable. A raspy voice growled, "Hey there, sweet meat, you want some sugar?"

I kept on walking.

"Hey, Mr. Red Pants, Mr. Little Red Riding Hood Pants, I'm talking to you, honey."

With that, I stopped dead in my tracks. They had to be talking to me. No one else on Sixth Avenue had Little Red Riding Hood pants on. Trembling, I turned slowly, losing my serious model glare, and I saw three of the most stereotypical New York City hookers in classic *Sweet Charity* poses, staring me up and down. They looked as if they had just walked off the set of *Baretta*.

"Come on, baby, we won't charge you that much."

Now visibly shaking and almost unable to speak, I stammered, "I-I-I beg your pardon?"

"Ooooh, chile, this motherfucker got manners."

"Ummm, I, ahhh, well, I don't think so, thank you

anyway," I managed to mutter as I turned to make a rapid exit.

"Maybe you don't like dark and lovely girls, is that it, baby? You don't want my brown sugar?"

Not wanting to offend her, and not knowing if they had weapons—not that they would need them, since I was as street-savvy as a debutante—I said quickly, "No, ma'am, that's not it at all, actually I prefer . . . the uh . . . brown sugar, but I've got to bring these sandwiches to my grandmother."

The moment I said this, I realized that I *was* Little Red Riding Hood, as did my dark and lovely ladies of the night. They screamed with laughter as I ran away as fast as I could, and in the distance I heard her holler, "That's okay, baby, I'll take a rain check—and welcome to New York Motherfuckin' City, have a nice day!"

Mom's on Five

By JANUARY of my sophomore year of high school at my beloved Newman School, I had evolved into a complete preppy, wearing colorful wide-wale corduroy pants even in the languid heat and humidity of New Orleans, Lacoste shirts under my oxford button-down, monogrammed starched shirts, penny loafers, and needle-pointed belts. Nothing, especially the elements, was going to stop my fashion drive. The look was safe and accepted in the Deep South in 1979, and at that point in my life, that was all I wanted. I continued to be my mom's secret fashion adviser, though, and with her I was anything but conservative, pushing for a high-fashion *Vogue* look in every aspect of her appearance.

My advice was paying off. For the first time in ages, her hair was capable of actual movement and, she confided in me, she felt attractive—and noticed by Dad and other men. A few months earlier, the Saks Fifth Avenue catalog arrived at home while Mom was in New York City accompanying Jay to his postgraduate year at the Lawrenceville School in

New Jersey. This arrival was second only in anticipation and importance to that of the September issue of *Vogue*. I immediately called her to describe the outfit on the cover that she just had to have: a perfect fall-toned silk foulard paisley. She did buy it, claiming Dad would kill her when he got the bills. The next day, she wore the stunning Anne Klein silk suit and Calvin Klein heels. Walking down Fifth Avenue with her, my brother was so stunned by some of the stares she received that he exclaimed, "Mom, did you see that? That man totally checked you out! No, really, top-to-bottom checked you out!"

Even better, she wore the same ensemble for her flight home. Walking with confidence, she passed right by Dad in the airport terminal. He did a double-take, saying, "Baby, is that you?"

Though she remained gracious and feminine, Mom had transformed herself inside and out. Her makeup, hair, and clothes had been updated, but so had her self-confidence. She knew it and loved it, saying to me several times, "Until you learn to love yourself, you really can't love anyone else." Dad's health had also taken a turn for the better, and their relationship seemed much improved and more secure than it had been during the last few tumultuous years. Though my stomach turned a little whenever I saw their increasing displays of physical affection—the lingering kisses, pats on the tush, snuggles in front of the television set—I knew it was a good thing, especially for Mom. Finally, she was in the best of all possible places.

Then, late that fall, Mom was scheduled for a "procedure" and had to spend the night in Baptist Hospital. She primped and packed her valise, and as I left for school, my parents told me to call the hospital at lunch or during my free period. The time came, and I called as requested, with no worries whatsoever. When I was connected to her room, Dad answered, and I noticed something strange in his voice, something I'd never heard before. He was crying. Nothing could have shaken me more.

"Daddy, what's the matter, tell me," I gasped.

"Your mother, she . . ."

"What? Tell me!" I screamed, to the surprise of everyone in the Newman library.

"It's cancer, son. Your mom has breast cancer." And with that he broke down, as did I. I knew virtually nothing about the disease, as it simply was not discussed back then, but I knew it had to be very, very bad if my big, strong dad was crumbling. He handed the phone to Moozie.

"Tomato, come over here," she said. "I'm sure your mother would love to see your sweet face when she comes out of recovery. I don't understand, she said the mammogram was benign, and now this. Oh God, why couldn't it have been me?" she cried. "I'm old and she . . . oh, my baby, just come on over here."

Panicked, I fled the library and asked my buddies David and Gordon to tell my teachers that I wouldn't be in class that afternoon as I had to rush over to the hospital. Jumping into my silver-blue Monte Carlo, I sped through the streets of Uptown New Orleans to Baptist Hospital, trying desperately not to cry. As a diversion I turned on the radio, but the Bee-Gees' hit "Tragedy" was playing, so I shut the radio off with such force that the tuning knob broke off in my hand. Breathlessly, I made it to the information desk, got my mom's room number, and took off quickly down the corridor, literally bumping into my cousin Debbie, now a nurse at the hospital, as I recklessly turned a corner.

I was on the verge of tears. "Debbie, how's Mom? Dad and Moozie were crying on the phone. What the hell is going on?"

Debbie rolled her eyes, then hugged me, saying, "Oh, they are just overreacting, sweetie. Breast cancer is not necessarily fatal. Many people survive, and early detection is important. The doctors will know more in a few days, when the lab reports on the lymph nodes come back. Now hurry on up, they're expecting you. Room 510, take a left out the elevator. And Bryan, keep your chin up and think positive."

Think positive? All I could think was my mother was going to die and why couldn't someone just tell me she was going to be okay? I entered the somber hospital suite and was greeted by Moozie, Aunt Vilma, and Mom's dear friend always known to us as Aunt Carol. She had made a hasty retreat from a luncheon at Commander's Palace as soon as she heard the news and informed me that Dad was in recovery with Mom. Carol, still wearing her signature oversized picture hat, had passed by Chopin's Florist on the way and had them create an enormous arrangement of roses and stargazer lilies, Mom's favorite, which she was placing on a table when she caught my eye. She ran to give me a kiss, but as usual her hat required expert maneuvering before contact could be made. She said softly, "Darling, you are an angel. Say a prayer for your mother. Remember, all things are possible with God."

Then I noticed her friend Dotty Brennan making her bed, not with sterile hospital sheets, but rather with her own exquisite satin and lace-trimmed bedding. Above the bed was a big "Get Well" sign obviously purchased from the hospital gift shop, with a piece of posterboard taped underneath, saying, "We Love You Gayle!"

Aunt Carol followed my gaze and said in her Virginia accent, "I thought the room needed some fixing, something to hopefully cheer your mother up. You know, a personal touch!" Carol, like my mother, was always trying to make others happy.

Just then, Dad entered the room, his eyes glassy, and immediately walked over to me and hugged me so hard I thought I'd break. Just for a moment, I could feel him quake as if he would cry, but the moment had passed by the end of our embrace. Moozie, eager for news, couldn't wait another moment before asking, "How is she, John? When can I see my baby girl?"

Dad took a deep breath and then another, forcing his giant hands into his khaki pants. "She's resting fine, she'll be up soon. The doctors had to perform a radical mastectomy."

Both Carol and Moozie gasped as he continued. "They are hopeful that they got it all and that the reports from her lymph nodes will come back negative. Next week they want to perform a complete hysterectomy because there is a possibility that the cancer could travel there."

Dad just hung his head, and this time I hugged him as hard as I could.

"Dammit to hell," Moozie moaned, breaking down, "why not me? Why not me? I'm old."

Dad called Jay on the phone and told him the news. He made plans to be back in New Orleans soon. By then, Mom's waiting room was filled with family and friends, including Oralea, who beckoned me over to her side. I had grown taller than her years ago, as her osteoporosis had caused her to hunch over. But she reached up and hugged me, saying, "Listen, Your Majesty, I know how much you love your mama, we all do. This ain't gonna be easy, I guarantee, but we can beat it. I've seen it done before. I got your favorite red beans and rice waiting for you at home, now show me a smile . . . I mean it, show me your smile . . . Good, and keep it on your face every time you go in and see your beautiful mama."

Minutes later, Mom was brought back from recovery, still a bit groggy from the anesthesia and in shock from the unexpected news of her mastectomy. One by one, we went into the adjoining bedroom. When it was my turn, she said, "Hey, pumpkin, how's my handsome young man?"

Seeing her hooked up to drips and drains, with barely a trace of color in her face, was too much for me. Holding her hand, I started to well up.

"Now honey," she said, "don't you fret, no sirree, I am going to be fine. When I was twelve years old I had a ruptured appendix, and peritonitis set in, do you know what that is?"

I shook my head.

"Well, it's poison, and it nearly killed me, but it didn't get me because I had to be here to have you and your brother, and I'm not leaving until I'm done with you two, and that's not for a long time. Now pet, I need you to be strong for your daddy. He needs you now, all right? Now give me some sugar." With that, I kissed her forehead and left.

More visitors kept arriving—the Brennans, the Nunguessers, the Watkinses, the Weilbachers—bringing wine and finger sandwiches, turning the waiting area into a bit of a cocktail party. I asked everyone questions about Mom's future: Dad, Debbie, Aunt Mid, and Aunt Vee. But no one had any concrete answers, or at least not the ones I wanted, and it was driving me insane. "It's in God's hands" and "We'll have to wait and see" were just not cutting it. I stormed out of the now-crowded lounge, down the fluorescent-lit, highly polished linoleum-tiled corridor to the charge nurse seated behind the desk. "Excuse me, my name is Bryan Batt, I am Gayle Batt's son, and I need to speak with her doctor as soon as possible!"

The nurse recoiled and stared at me, as if to ask, *Who do you think you are?*

But before she could utter a word, I felt a gentle touch upon my shoulder, and turning around I came face to face with Dr. Sebastian, her surgeon.

"I need to know, I need to know, and nobody has any answers. You are her doctor. Please tell me something, anything."

"Young man," he said calmly, with kind authority, "this is not usually done, but since I know your mother would want me to, okay."

He put his arm around my shoulder as he walked me down the hall.

"Now son, I am going to be honest. You are old enough for the truth. Your mother had a serious procedure, and we had to remove one of her breasts because there was a cancerous tumor inside. We also removed some lymph nodes for testing. If the lymph nodes prove negative, then your mother's situation will be much better. I believe that we got it all and that the tests will come back negative, but we have to wait a few days for the results. Do you think you can you hang in there until then?"

I nodded. "So if those tests come back negative, then she'll be fine, right?"

"Well, son, it's not as easy as all that," he went on. "You see, if those results come back negative, then there is a very good chance it didn't spread, but there are other tests we have to do to make sure it's not traveled to any other organs in her body. If all those tests come back negative, that's good too. But the rule is five years cancer-free before patients are considered cured."

Dr. Sebastian was paged over the loudspeaker, and he patted my shoulder gently with his manicured hands before leaving me alone at the end of the hall. What would I do if my mother died? Because of my father's heart condition, I always feared that he might die, but I had never, ever thought about losing my mother so soon.

To OUR GREAT RELIEF, all the test results came back negative and her lymph nodes were clear. However, ten days after her initial surgery, she underwent a hysterectomy. Then, as if all of that weren't enough, she had a subcutaneous mastectomy on her remaining breast. Mom entered the hospital at the pinnacle of feminine beauty, but within a month she walked out a butchered and completely altered person. No matter how she tried, she would never be able to lose the nearly twenty pounds she gained in the hospital due to the change in her hormone levels—and perhaps to the rich New Orleans food that friends and family lavished on her. All in all, she would never physically be the same again. But her face, her dancing, twinkling eyes and stunning smile, remained, as did her indomitable spirit.

That spirit would be tested again and again in the coming years, years filled with more and more illness and fear. Mom underwent two grueling and painful reconstructive surgeries as well as three more resulting from her body's reaction to the implants.

Meanwhile, Dad's heart continued to falter severely as he drank more heavily. Finally his doctor informed Mom that he was indeed killing himself with alcohol. Never missing a step, Mom sought a nearby treatment center in Baton Rouge, and twice a week we would drive for our coaching sessions on how to perform an intervention. Mom was fully prepared to leave him if he did not agree to go to the treatment center after we confronted him with how his drinking had negatively affected our lives. Fortunately, he agreed to go. And with only a few slips, Dad remained sober for the rest of his life. But it was indeed too late; the damage to his heart and other vital organs was irreversible.

Two months after his release, just short of Mom's two-year mark of being cancer-free, a tiny malignant tumor was discovered and removed just under the skin of what remained of her left breast. By this point Dad was in and out of the hospital constantly, a huge oxygen tank was kept in the den, and everyone in the household had taken a course in CPR. The recurrence of Mom's cancer was the worst possible news. There are many words I hate, and although *hate* itself has become one of them, it appropriately describes my deep sentiments surrounding the words *malignant, metastasize,* and *recurrence.*

Mom made a trip to the M. D. Anderson Cancer Center in Houston for a complete evaluation, and upon returning she announced her plan to the family. She had stopped at Neiman Marcus in the Galleria Mall, and I was proud that without my help, Mom had selected a stunning ensemble all on her own. We all sat on the massive L-shaped chocolate leather sofas that faced the vintage brick hearth—Dad, Jay, Moozie, Oralea, and me—as Mom made her presentation with an air of confidence.

"Okay, my loves, here's the deal. The sweet doctors at M. D. Anderson ran every test possible, every fancy kind of X-ray, on every fancy advanced machine on the planet. And thank God, they could not find a trace of the cancer anywhere. That's the good news . . . Hooray!" She shook her bejeweled hands over her head in a "praise the Lord" gesture. Whenever the phrase "good news" was used, I knew bad news was right around the corner. She continued, her voice as lovely as always but stronger and more determined.

"I asked them what they would recommend for treatment, and the doctors said full radiation and chemotherapy. So I said, 'Okey-dokey, let me get this straight. There is no cancer detectable in my entire body, yet you want to blast me full of toxic chemicals and radiate me to boot?' " She was on a roll, acting out the exchange both physically and vocally, imitating the Texan twang on top of her own lilting drawl.

"'Hm-hmm, that's correct, Mrs. Batt.' So I asked what they would have for me if in fact the dirty little rascal came back to visit again, and they said, 'Well, then, we would have to use a lesser treatment.' So I said thank you very much, and that I would let them know my decision. Now y'all, I have thought and thought about this. Maybe this tiny recurrence was a fluke and not related to the last cancer spell. Why pull out the heavy artillery now? Wouldn't it make sense to bomb when attacked? So I've decided to take a pill that has been shown to help keep the kind of cancer I had at bay. But wait, there's more. On the plane ride home, I sat next to a lady who was coming back from M. D. Anderson as well. We started to chat, and she pulled out small containers of her own food, and I asked her what it was. She explained that she was on a macrobiotic diet, and it had been proven that it helped fight cancer. She said that we are ingesting a lot of chemicals and preservatives in our diet that cancer just loves. She also gave me names of books to read and groups that teach creative and healing visualization and so on. So here's the deal, I am going on that diet and I am going to every class I can and beat this. Then if one day I have to do the chemo, so be it—no Gayle!"

She stopped and corrected herself as if admonishing a small child. "Take that back, take that thought back from the universe!" She reached out and grabbed the air in front of her and tossed the imaginary thought over her shoulder. Mom inhaled a big, deep breath and continued for a moment with her eyes closed. "You are a healthy and healing child of God." She quickly opened her eyes wide, explaining, "That is what is called an affirmation. Cheryl, the lady on the plane, said it's all about positive thinking and seeing yourself well, mind over matter. So that's it, kiddos, I am now off to a little grocery on Esplanade called the Whole Food Company. They sell only organic and chemical-free food. I think we will have some free-range chicken tonight, and steamed vegetables and kale. Any questions?"

Our mouths ajar, we could only look at one another in silent shock. "No? All righty, then."

She kissed us each as she made her way to the door, collecting her handbag and notepad from the plane ride. With each kiss we smiled slightly, not knowing what to say. "Family, I am off to the Beacon Bookstore, then to make an appointment at the Agape Center, and finally a pass by the Whole Food Company. Oralea, I'll be back in about an hour and a half. Would that give us enough time to fix a healthy dinner? Oooh, and brown rice too?"

Oralea nodded. *"Oui, Madame,* I hear you loud and clear!"

As Mom hurried out the side door, Dad, stunned, muttered, "Jesus Anthony Christ."

Jay shook his head. "They obviously didn't do a brain scan, because Mom has lost it!"

Moozie and I sat completely still, not knowing whether to laugh or cry.

Oralea marched front and center, put her hands in her white uniform pockets, and grinned from ear to ear. "You gentlemen can say what you want, but Miss Gayle's done put her boxing gloves on. That is the sign of a woman in love. She in love with her family and she in love with life and you just can't mess with that, no way, no how. I guarantee, that lady is going to outlive us all, they are going to have to drag her kicking and screaming from this world. Oooooh, that's my girl. Now excuse me, I got to make a few calls and find out what the dickery-dock is brown rice and how do you cook it!"

AND SO IT was that Mom stayed faithful to her macrobiotic diet, bringing Tupperware containers of brown rice and seaweed to the best restaurants in town and continually perplexing waiters by requesting steamed vegetables and poached fish—Creole cuisine blasphemy. Miraculously, it worked, but as always, with the good news came the bad. Dad's situation continued to worsen. There were countless trips in the ambulance to the hospital, and he grew so weary of the ordeal. He was diagnosed with premature ventricular contractions, which would throw his weakened and enlarged heart into fibrillation, for which there was no treatment or cure at the time. Mom saw that we had a defibrillator in the home, and educated herself on exactly what medications were needed to stabilize him if such an attack occurred. Her desire to hold on to the man she loved was unswerving, and although he was finally brought home because he didn't want to die in the hospital, she never surrendered her hope.

Mom called all over the South and the entire country to find doctors who might have any trial or experimental treatments. Nothing. The last attempt was to be a heart transplant; this rarely successful operation was the only possibility left. It appeared that there was a doctor in California who would perform the surgery, and Mom clung to that tiny sliver of hope with every fiber of her soul, but finally the call came that Dad was not a viable candidate. Although she begged the doctor to try anyway, it was to no avail. Mom then gave up, but not completely. She later told me that she ran into her boudoir and collapsed, crying, ranting to the heavens.

"I GIVE UP, DO YOU HEAR ME? I GIVE UP! YOU WIN! There is nothing else I can do, so I am turning it over to you. I've done everything possible . . . It's your will . . . not mine!"

The very next day there was a call from Dr. Albert Hyman, a heart specialist from right there in New Orleans. He informed my mother that there was a new heart medication that was garnering great results, and although it had not yet been approved by the FDA, he was able to procure the drug for Dad as an experimental trial. There was a fifty percent chance it would work, with jaundice as a possible side effect. The medication worked, and for the next five years they lived as newlyweds. From being bedridden, he was able to take Mom to dinner, have weekend visits to the Coast with all their fun friends, and dance at the thirtieth-anniversary party Jay and I threw them on October 10, 1985. Given a similar high school home life, I wouldn't blame a kid for running as far as he could for college. I chose to stay in my own backyard, and never regretted that decision.

Our fraternal grandmother, Mom-ee, had passed away the summer prior, and left Jay and me a small sum to travel abroad. I had used a little of mine to move up to New York in September to pursue my dream of being an actor. So instead of a European tour, we chose to throw a lavish fête for our parents and reunite their wedding party. Knowing that Dad would not hear of such an extravagance, we decided to make it a surprise, but Moozie informed us that Mom would just have a fit if she didn't have time to get the right dress, and that we shouldn't do anything to suddenly shock Dad. So we compromised, and both Mom and Dad received the invitation when all their family and friends did. Dad called me, reeling. "Are you boys out of your minds? You can't afford this kind of party right now; you are just starting out in life."

Jay and I had rehearsed our response. "Dad, one day we will be able to afford this, but we don't know what the future holds, so we are doing it now."

The event was fantastic. Friends from all over the country flew in, and as he went to bed that night he said to Mom, "I just can't sleep, Gayle, tonight was just so wonderful. . . . We have two wonderful sons."

He leaned over to kiss her, smiling and saying softly, "I have you to thank for that."

One month later, almost to the day, Dad died in his sleep. He was fifty-five years old.

Don't Cry for Me
Akron, Ohio

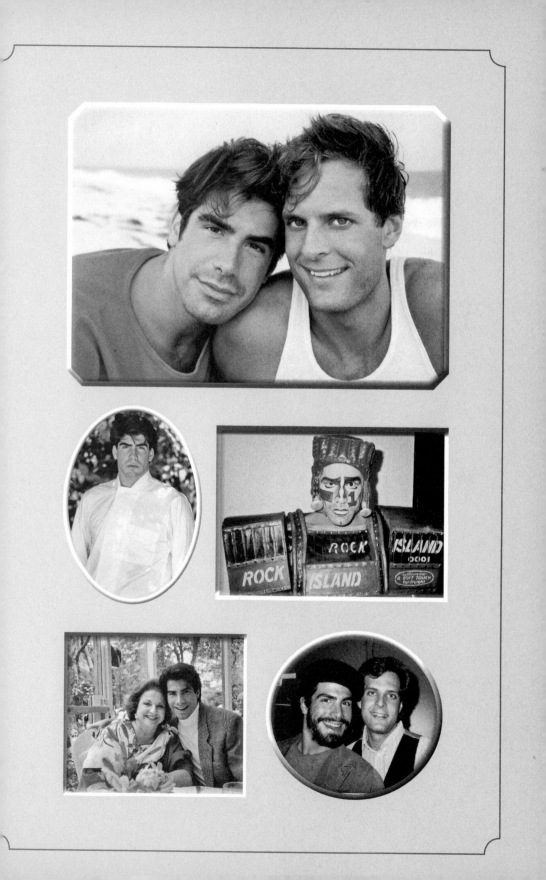

My ONE DREAM, my single goal, was to be in a Broadway show, and now it was finally happening. So what if it was *Starlight Express,* Andrew Lloyd Webber's monstrously overproduced mega-musical retelling of "The Little Engine That Could"? And I was dressed as a train with five-pound roller skates on each foot, singing and dancing a grueling routine on a massive three-story "train set" complete with illuminated Plexiglas bridges, tunnels, drops, and bowls? And so what if the show received some of the most scathing reviews in theatrical history? I was on Broadway! I loved every moment of it, especially working with the cast and, as a principal, having my own dressing room, with my bio and picture in the *Playbill*. But mostly I loved the sense of belonging I felt every time I walked through the stage door. I have never tired of that glorious sensation, and pray that I never will.

To celebrate my Broadway debut, Mom invited all of our family and friends to New York to see me in the show, followed by a post-theatre dinner at the Russian Tea Room. Since she never had a daughter to officially launch into the world with a proper "coming out," Gayle treated this night as a sort of debut party for me. It wasn't the typical white-dress-and-curtsey debut, but it was a debut none-theless, and she was not going to let this once-in-a-lifetime moment pass without the proper attention it deserved. Mom spared no expense; she had custom invitations created with the all-too-precious wording "They say the starlight sure shines bright . . . *ON BROADWAY*!" About three dozen family members and family friends came up en masse for the event. After the matinee, the house manager of the Gershwin Theater knocked on my dressing room door, saying, "Bryan, I don't know if you realize this, but there is a large group of people waiting in the lobby. I believe your mother is here with quite a few ladies, and they all have on furs."

"I am so sorry, Rick," I said. "I told her over and over to come to the stage door. Is there any way I could take them on set for a quick tour?"

"I think this will be the largest group ever, but all right."

I brought all of them up on stage, to the elation of Moozie and Donna and her daughter Whitney, one of my seven sweet godchildren. As I pointed out the dangers and mechanics of the treacherous set, I looked over at Mom, beaming with joy as she spoke with the Watkins twins. Some photos were taken, and as the tour was coming to an end and as I was showing everyone to the elevator and stairwell, my dad's best friend who just happens to be Aunt Carol's husband, Uncle Jack put his arm around me and said, "You know, your daddy would be so proud of you. You did this all on your own. Nobody could make a call or set this up, you did it, and no one can take that away from you. It's rare to get to live your dream." He paused for a second, then went on, "Did I tell you the one about the rabbi, the priest, and the Baptist?"

"No, Uncle Jack . . . but thank you."

In college I had grown quite inclusive and loved making friends from all walks of life, from all cultural backgrounds, and while some of my friends only ran with their "set," I couldn't wait to meet different people, artistic people— actors, musicians, writers, and more. Mom knew that this would not just be a little social debut, but my real debut, and the invitation list reflected this promise, New Orleans meets Broadway. Cocktails and wine flowed like the Mississippi. If there is one thread that ties my taste in friends together, it is the love of a good time and the ability to celebrate, so after the Russian Tea Room all that were willing joined the caravan of cabs to my one-bedroom flat, where we danced the night away. Yes, threats to call the police were made by my neighbors, and finally, by Tuesday night's performance, my hangover had kindly released me from its agonizing clutches.

One year later, the train had derailed—*Starlight Express* was closing. After the final performance, I rolled down the linoleum corridors and climbed up two flights of stairs on my rubber toe stops, with tears rolling down my ridiculously painted face. It had been a magical year. Even tearing the cartilage in my knee during my second-act number, followed by surgery and six weeks of recovery, seemed a small price to pay for the thrill of being a part of this show, but now it was all over and I was inconsolable.

Jane Krakowski, who played Dinah the dining car, did her best to comfort me, assuring me there would be other shows. Although she was only nineteen years old at the time, she had a wealth of experience in show business and had already been nominated for a daytime Emmy for her moving portrayal of T. R. Kendall on *One Life to Live*. I appreciated her sage showbiz advice, but I also had a closet crush on her and secretly wished that we could date. But Jane had been around the theatrical block before, and intuitively knew in which direction my preferences *really* went.

Although I desperately tried to keep my desires hidden, it was clear to many people that I was just knock, knock, knockin' on the closet door. I constantly tried to suppress my undeniable attraction to men, and frequently as well as willingly lost the battle. Yet I was able to find beautiful, virtuous young ladies to date and share enjoyable yet alcohol-induced relations, but these liaisons were fireworks free. At the ripe age of twenty-four, I somehow attracted young women to beard. I didn't know any better. This little deception was all well and good for a while because I truly couldn't fathom an "out" gay life.

Instead, after a climax-free hetero date and an ample dose of vodka, this handsome young buck would don a pair of tight Levi's and hit The Works, a gay bar on Columbus Avenue. I'd amble in trembling with desire, fear, lust, and raging guilt, but nothing could stop me. No matter how I tried to reverse my tracks, my feet had wings and led me closer. Within minutes of entering the dark bar and a few pounding strains of "Relax" by Frankie Goes to Hollywood, eye contact would be made, followed by a smile and a slinky exit to his place. I never revealed my real name. There are quite a few willing men who may fondly remember a midnight tryst with the elusive and tipsy Brad, Rick, or Craig.

These lurid encounters were often thrilling and for an instant satisfying, but then the waves upon waves of fear and guilt, guilt and fear would hit. I'd daydream nightmarish scenarios of jealous lovers "outing me" to my shocked and unsuspecting mother and family in the middle of a packed Galatoire's restaurant on a Sunday evening where everyone knew everyone, including those who were at my Russian Tea Room debut, and all would be horrified. Even Nelson, our family waiter, would shake his head in disbelief and disdain as he handed my sobbing mother a freshly pressed white linen napkin and served the piping hot soufflé potatoes. Being outed seemed a fate worse than death; coming out was utterly unimaginable.

Until then, I never knew people in real gay relationships. Like so many, I never had a role model. And one can't really count ponytailed and bronze-blushed George, Mom's ex-hairdresser turned wardrobe supervisor for Siegfried and Roy. (Let's be honest, after coiffing Gayle, really where else was he to turn?) My biggest fear was that I was doomed to live the rest of my life alone and, worse, loveless.

Jane, prudent beyond her years, and gifted with an understanding soul, told me that I could be anything I wanted to be and love anyone I wanted to. She also advised me to save some money from my paycheck each week, as actors never knew when the next job was going to appear. Foolishly, I didn't listen to her and thought the show would never close, and that once on Broadway, always on Broadway. Big mistake!

Once the show did close, it would be weeks before I could collect my much-needed unemployment benefits, and I had vowed, since my father's untimely passing, never to burden my mother with my financial woes. So, reluctantly, I called my former employer to eat crow and, if necessary, beg her to give me back my old job as a "fragrance model," the lowest rung on the modeling ladder, at Bloomingdale's, the Ringling Brothers of retail. I was paid to obnoxiously invade innocent customers' personal space and force them, with a plastic smile affixed to my face, to sample the latest designer aromas—perfumes, eau de toilettes, and every imaginable crème, gel, or body douche—and sell, sell, and sell. It's not that ghastly, once you come to terms with embarrassment and degradation. The pay is decent, the hours are flexible so there's time to go to auditions, and samples abound so that my friends and I always smelled clean, spicy, or musky, depending on the vendor.

Fortunately, they took me back, and on my first day I was warmly greeted by a few of the same co-workers who had bid me adieu for the lights of Broadway just a year ago. Eric, a fleshy, aging twink with an overly high and low-lighted bleached blond wedge haircut, was the exception. This egomaniacal poof referred to himself in the third person as Mr. Eric, and worse, he was a self-absorbed, self-proclaimed expert on all aspects of the business of "show," from Hell's Kitchen gossip to cutting-edge MTV pop music trivia:

"Mr. Eric thinks little Miss Whitney thing is fierce, girl" . . . "Patty Lupone, ooh, don't make Mr. Eric go there, chile, unless you want a pyrotechnical display, the diva can sing down."

Every clichéd statement was buttoned with the hackneyed triple snap. He wore so heavily on everyone's nerves, but especially on mine. He was out, open, and free. He was himself. He frightened me. He saddened me. He made me wonder what my life would become. Fear fueled by fear.

In all fairness, I have to admit, he did have some semblance of wit, which I envied. When a new perfume line, like Dior's Poison, was being launched and the main drag of the fragrance promenade was completely carpeted in purple plush, with wild green and golden vines wrapped around every column, I and the other part-time retail sheep would follow the strict pitch lines and approach dictated by both Bloomie's and the Christian Dior reps. Not Mr. Eric:

"Ladies, be the first on your block to Poison your husband, the newest and hottest fragrance from the one and only legendary fashion icon Christian Dior, introducing Poison. It's to die for!"

"Try some Poison?"

"May I Poison you, ma'am?"

What rankled most was that people lapped it up. He was a success. Meanwhile, I just sucked in my cheeks to give the appearance of sculpted cheekbones like a real model and ask if passersby would care to try this new stuff called Poison. The more he hawked, the more I tried the sexy soft sell. The more flamboyantly he raved, the more pantherlike I posed.

And as the day progressed, and I became a mannequin in response to Mr. Eric's fabulousness, the Dior reps asked me to be more clever and energetic in my sales approach, to "say and spray" more like Mr. Eric. All day, all I heard was Mr. Eric, Mr. Eric, Mr. Eric.

Just as the day was thankfully crawling to an end, Lorna of the Bloomie's fragrance brass sauntered to my side. She was an emaciated, painfully platinum permed woman with a disturbingly crinkled Louis Vuitton Bocca tan, which had prematurely aged her bitter rainbow-painted face. Why is it that people in the cosmetics sales business find the need to wear as many possible shades of eye shadow, blush, and lipstick all at the same time, as if they were a living display palette? Lorna was the rule rather than the exception. Her motto was "More is more, and it's not done until it is over-done." Whatever the trend du jour was, she raped it. Fresh from her Virginia Slims cigarette break, which was every fifteen minutes, she graveled, "Bry baby, the frog fags at Dior think you're cute, but they're not having your 'subtle' approach at all what-so-ev-a, and to tell you the shit, nei-ther am I. So tomorrow I'm switching you to Perry Ellis, and pep it up or it's bye-bye Bloomie's, hello Della Caravag-gio House of Pasta, you get the drift, toots. See you tomor-row, and wear something Perry Ellissy—and tight. Ciao bella, I mean bello, wink, wink, kiss, kiss, whateva."

The next day I wore aubergine pleated trousers and a black turtleneck under a signature plaid Perry Ellis blazer—in fact it was the very one from his fall ad campaign, the last collection he designed before he died from AIDS. Thank God for the "sample sale" industry, which would not only clothe me in the latest styles at a fraction of the cost, but would also allow me more flexible hours of employment stocking racks upon racks, assisting incredibly rude, fashion-challenged people's decisions, and keeping the wig-wearing garmento wives from killing each other and everyone else at the dreaded Escada sale.

Walking to Bloomie's, as if I were walking the Perry Ellis runway, a skill I had mastered years ago by studying the fashion show videotapes in the designer sections of Rubenstein Brothers of New Orleans, I pondered possible pitches to impress Lorna and other cosmetic hags. My primary aim, though, was to outshine Mr. Eric. *They want pizzazz, they're going to get it,* I thought.

I galloped onto the perfumery gallery at peak stride, and executed a perfect one-and-a-half Dior turn, then dramatically snapped my head east, fixing my now smoldering eyes on Lorna. "Mr. B's the name, fragrance is the game."

Impressed by my newfound self-confidence and runway prowess, Lorna, stifling an emphysemic hack, growled, "Better, bubee, love the way the hair keeps moving even after you've stopped, now that's talent, my fried mop is so plastered with that stiff stuff shit it's about to break off, and then what? Yours truly will look like a Chernobyl gerbil with a tan, God forbid." I rattled off my new pitch lines:

"The fashion, the flair, the style, the scent, it's essential Ellis for men."

"Sample the casual elegance that is the world of Perry Ellis."

"Perry is sooooooo *very*."

Lorna pointed to the door and exclaimed, "Get out there and spray, baby, spray!"

Now on a male fragrance-model high, without even inhaling the aromatic fumes, I strutted my cookies out to the bustling Bloomie's cosmetic drag, turning on a dime, flipping and working my newfound best attribute—my hair.

My long bangs were still in motion when I spotted Mr. Eric. He was working, of all designers, Calvin. Calvin Klein! The be-all and end-all of American contemporary design. Calvin redefined fashion, invented the camel-toe designer jean, brought back the bomber jacket, and, of course, Calvin, his classic first male fragrance in the navy blue streamlined bottle, my signature, which I was wearing right then, and perhaps too much of it. I liked Perry's scent, but it really was too sweet, for me, and even though "Calvin" was a bit musky, the touch of citrus made it a classic. I did know my designer colognes.

Mr. Eric was standing there head to toe in the newest Calvin Klein triumph of design—draped beige. Before it was black, black, black, and then draped beige. Calvin is so revolutionary. Mr. Eric looked me up and down, and grinned, because he knew I was perfect Perry, and he was cookie-cutter Calvin.

"Sample the casual elegance that is the world of Calvin Klein."

That was my line, dammit. Literally. I had come up

with that simple yet poignant catchphrase, and in the blink of an eye, I had been robbed.

With eyes burning, I shot back with his line, "Ladies, be the first on your block to poison your man with Perry Ellis."

Not realizing what I had said, or that it made no sense, I repeated it over and over just to taunt Mr. Eric. A small group started to assemble in my area as I grew more animated, raising my voice to shout even more inappropriate slogans. Finally Mr. Eric tried to subtly correct me. I don't know what I was thinking, but I just sauntered away from him with a runway turn, and announced to the crowd as their jaws dropped, "Try Perry Ellis, the man is gone but his fragrance lingers." That definitely didn't come out right.

A few audible gasps, a "Well, I never," and that was the end of my modeling career. Lorna, shaking her finger and head at the same time in a gesture far too physically complex to describe, moaned, "You were good, Brybubee, ya didn't know any better, a babe in the woods, there are sharks out there, tootsie, sharks that will cut you down and serve you for hors d'oeuvres. But one word of advice— make that several—never degrade deceased designers, I know it was not your intention, you are a pussycat, but just the same I've got three Ellis brass fuming in the rest area behind Chloe, and one wants to see you outside, so my suggestion is go out the door you came in, sweetie, take some samples, and good luck in your playacting. Go!"

And so I did. I walked north back to my lonely abode away from the Bloomingdale's palace, questioning everything in my life. How could it have come to this? How could I let that guy get to me? What will I do for a job? I would not call my mom for money. Only the fresh green stupidity of youth kept my stride from faltering. At home I threw myself onto my eternally unmade single bed, only to see the message light flashing. Maybe the Ellis estate was taking legal action, maybe Betsy Bloomingdale was on her way to chew me out herself; I'd read in *W* that she could be brutal. I wearily reached over and pressed the button, the relentlessly blinking button. Danger.

Beep. ". . . No, Oralea dawlin', that goes in the attic . . . hello Bryan . . . Dawlin' . . . are you there . . . Pick up if you are theeeere . . . Oh I Sewanee, I'll never get used to these things. Anyhoo pumpkin-eater boy, how'd your audition go for *Evita,* I know you would love to play that part of Shay or Che-Che, I never can remember the name of that character, and I know how much you want it, you'd be perfect . . . By the bye, sweetie, are you still taking your voice lessons regularly and going to Alice's acting class, you've got to keep on studying, well, give me a call . . . Oralea sends her love . . . and can't wait to see you on Broadway again . . . Oralea, this show is for dinner theatre in Ohio, not Broadway . . . Oralea says she still can't wait to see you on Broadway again . . . neither can I, but I'll come to Akron just the same, love you my heart."

Beep. "Bryan, it's Barbara Sanders calling from Honey Sanders's office . . . your agent, sorry it's been so long, but . . . NO . . . tell them no . . . no . . . over my dead body will he go back into *Cats* FOR LESS MONEY, AIN'T GONNA HAPPEN! SHUT UP TELL ANDREW LLOYD WEBHEAD HE CAN CALL ME COLLECT . . . Doll, it's some good news. You got it! Che in *Evita,* you'll have to grow a beard, but hey. Good cast. Sue Cella, who covered Patti on Broadway, will be Eva, and David Brummell, who did the tour, a dead ringer for Peron. The money is not Broadway, but it's a lead, you are young, and it's a great opportunity, so you'll do it. I already did the deal. Come sign your contract before you leave for Akron, Ohio, day after tomorrow, now I did get you star billing, star housing, though that ain't saying much. So way to go, remember one thing, kiddo, and I know I don't need to tell you this, be on time, keep your nose clean, don't make waves, that's what I'm here for, and try not to fish off the company pier, if you get my drift, it's always a bitch when you get back to the real world."

Salvation!

The next day two great college friends took me out for a birthday bon voyage dinner. Leslie Castay, who had moved to New York at the same time to become an actress, and David Pons, my fraternity little brother/young Elvis lookalike, marched me into the ever-thrifty Second Avenue Sezchuan Hunan Cottage II. It was the home of General Ching's chicken, prepared the very same way for Chairman Mao, and all the cheap rotgut box wine one could drink! Heaven. We laughed as we stumbled home and my unsuspecting friends chided that perhaps I'd meet Miss Right in Akron, crazier things have happened. All I knew was that I had to keep my secret safe; otherwise I would lose these dear friends as well as all my childhood, high school, and college friends whom I adored, not to mention my family. Too much to risk, so I bottled it up, with the bottle.

"Yeah, who knows, I love tall, wholesome blondes, and the Midwest is full of them, right?"

The next morning I was on the plane to Akron, Ohio, the Rubber Capital of the World, to play Che in *Evita*, a role I had longed to play for years. Seated next to me was a very stylish and accessorized lady who wore bright jewel tones and a large, low-slung eighties belt, tights, and ankle boots, and carried a Perry Ellis faux leopard coat. My kind of gal. Within a few moments we came to the realization that we were both in the show and she was Susan Cella, who would play Eva. She had many other credits, like the original companies of *On the Twentieth Century* and *Me and My Girl*. I was certainly impressed and somewhat intimidated.

Soon we would be settled in our temporary hotel rooms for a few days of rehearsal until the cast of Maury Yeston's *Phantom of the Opera* closed and moved out. Later we would move to the same depressing tract housing they had occupied, four units per structure all in a row, with parking in front and snow-covered woods in back. Thank God the principal players did not have to share bedrooms as the chorus members did, just the common areas of kitchen and living room. On our first night, there was a sort of impromptu get-together at the Carousel Dinner Theater, where we were to dine and see the show, or, as it came to be known, "chew and view." There was a lot of the noisy activity typical of theatre people arriving at a hotel, shrill screams of those who had worked together before, and lots of doors shutting and calls down the hall. I now started to understand why some hotels in the past had refused actors. Suddenly there was a knock at my door, and when I opened it, there stood a tall, lanky young man with a very handsome face and the most beautiful crystal blue eyes I'd ever seen. I was caught off guard for a moment, and he was as well. For a split second we just stood there looking at each other, until I said, "Hi, are you in the show?"

He answered quickly, "Um, yes, I am. Tom, Tom Cian-fichi. I'm in the ensemble and understudying Magaldi."

We both reached out our hands at the same time to shake, and they remained together unnoticed by either of us throughout our conversation. As much as I tried, I could not remember how he pronounced his last name.

"Uhhh, nice to meet you, I'm playing Che. I'm Bryan, Bryan Batt."

"That's great, great role . . . Uhhh . . . I was looking for a James Anderson, he's supposed to be my roommate, but I can't seem to find him."

"Sorry, Tom, but I've not met him yet."

We then noticed our hands and pulled them away. I quickly spoke to cover the awkward moment. "Are you going to see the show tonight? Uhhh, I was going to see if Sue wants to sit together, she's our *Eva,* been in a bunch of Broadway shows. I've only been in one, *Starlight Express.* You could sit with us."

"Sure, that sounds great, I'll find this James Anderson and get settled; see you at the van at six. Thanks."

"Sure, see you at the van. How seventies, right? Uhhh, see you at six."

I closed the door, and swore I could hear children sing-ing "The Hills Are Alive with the Sound of Music" just like the moment in the film of *The Sound of Music* when Captain Von Trapp is berating Maria for making play outfits from the old curtains for the children, then off in the distance their angelic voices are heard and his heart begins to melt. That was the feeling I was experiencing at the moment, new, wonderful, and frightening. Over the next two weeks of rehearsal we would hang out together, and finally, on opening night, April 1, 1989, after a few Casa Rosada Colada specialty drinks at the Carousel Dinner Theater's Brass Ring Bar, as we lagged behind the crowd through the dark backstage labyrinth, we shared a kiss. The next day Tom overheard one of the female members of the ensemble saying, "I think Bryan likes me," but he knew otherwise.

Over the next weeks and months of the run, we took walks, made each other dinners and breakfasts, and enjoyed the fun part of a burgeoning relationship, the discovery. The only problem was that I was still completely closeted and was terrified by the idea of anyone knowing my secret. I don't know how he put up with me through this period, which lasted a good year and a half, but amazingly he did. As the snow-covered land gave way to the greens of spring, and bright yellow forsythia blossomed, we grew closer together, and often covert clandestine trysts were arranged due to our spring fever. One day my housemate, Gibb Twitchell, who played Magaldi, was off to search antique malls in the surrounding area for his beloved Roseville pottery, an excursion that would take at least several hours. So quickly I called Tom over to visit. Just after the games had begun, I heard the front door open. Gibb had come back, and he called out, "Bryan, are you here? I decided not to go after all."

Tom froze as a look of unadulterated panic came over my heated face.

"I'll be right out, Gibb, just getting dressed."

Barely whispering I handed Tom his clothes and hurried him into the closet, whispering to him that I would let him know when the coast was clear to make an exit. I quickly jumped into my jeans and shoes, buttoning my oxford shirt as I nonchalantly sauntered out of my bedroom, "Gibb, I think I'll take a little walk, it's so beautiful out today," I said ever so casually as I made my way to the door, trying not to look back into my bedroom for traces of Tom. I quickly flew down the front plank stairs, and when I reached the parking lot which was our front yard, the idea came. I looked over my shoulder at the wooded area directly behind the row of housing and walked toward it, then suddenly let out a bloodcurdling scream.

"Oh my God, oh my God, look at that snake, I've never seen a snake that huge! Everyone come see, oh my God . . . Gibb! Sue! Everyone! What kind of snake is that?"

One by one the cast rushed to my side, looking for the serpent, some of the over-actors actually claiming to see the snake. When nearly everyone was in the back looking for the figment of my reptilian imagination, I noticed Tom coming down my steps to join the fray, and with a wink all was fine. We would encounter far more trying events and adversity, but an irrevocable bond had formed that would not be undone.

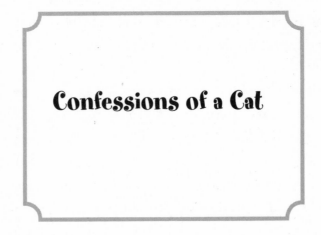

Confessions of a Cat

FROM DECEMBER OF 1990 until December of 1992 I was the biggest pussy on Broadway. For six months on the road plus a year and a half on Broadway, I was in the cast of *Cats*. Whatever cartilage I had left in my knees after my year roller-skating in *Starlight Express* was completely destroyed after this stint. And although my joints are shot and I can predict the weather with my left knee, I would not trade the thrill of having appeared in either of those Broadway extravaganzas for anything.

The Broadway company of *Cats* was approaching its ninth year when I eagerly and happily joined the troupe. Some of the original members or early replacements were still dancing in the litter box, and there were quite a number of bitter cast members who seriously needed attitude adjusting. Some of the more jaded leotard-clad felines actually felt as if they were doing management a favor by showing up to work. This bitchy attitude was completely lost on me. Yes, we were in a huge, long-running hit.

Yes, we were unrecognizable at the stage door. And yes, at this point our audiences were predominantly drowsy non-English-speaking tourists. (I am convinced they were shuttled directly from JFK airport to the Winter Garden Theater. When the lights dimmed they fell fast asleep, and it gave me great mischievous pleasure to startle them awake as I crawled through the audience reciting T. S. Eliot's "The Naming of Cats.") But I knew that the number of actors who would kill for this job would stretch around 51st Street, and so I acted accordingly—professionally and gratefully.

I looked to the late, great Laurie Beechman as an example. I had been a fan of Laurie's since I first saw her as the narrator in *Joseph and the Amazing Technicolor Dream Coat*. She was a pint-sized dynamo with a huge, spine-tingling voice and a kind, loving heart. She quickly became a dear friend and confidante to me as well as to Tom. When we met she was battling stage three ovarian cancer, which she would continue to fight for eight years. She simply amazed me with her strength, talent, and grace.

About nine months into my Broadway run, while Laurie brilliantly belted out the show's trademark song, "Memory," my eyes wandered into the audience. My gaze fell upon a grandmother, mother, and son, seated in the very same box seat that Mom, Moozie, and I shared at my first Broadway show some fifteen years before. I felt a warmth I'd never felt before, and as the months progressed, I would often look at that box and think of that magical, life-changing night so many years ago and of the storied history of this landmark theatre. *West Side Story,*

Mame, and *Funny Girl* all played in this beautiful temple to the gods of Comedy and Tragedy, which was now transformed into an oversized junkyard.

Although I was grateful for the part and well compensated, I was beginning to tire, body and soul. Dancing in eight performances a week was exhausting, and doing the claw-and-paw hand gestures and perfecting my tail-flicking technique were not satisfying my desire to be an actor. I continued with voice and acting classes, but I didn't want to act in my living room or a studio. I wanted to act on a stage, in a play, again.

After expressing this desire to my new agent, Bill Timms, at the agency I then referred to as IKEA of musical comedy because they signed everyone on Broadway, I soon had an audition scheduled for a new play by Paul Rudnick. I had seen Rudnick's play *I Hate Hamlet* a couple of years before on Broadway and thought it was hysterical. I was also impressed with the small off-Broadway theatre that was producing the new show. The WPA Theatre under the watch of Kyle Rennick had given audiences *Little Shop of Horrors* and *Steel Magnolias.* Who knew, I thought, maybe this new play, *Jeffrey,* could make it as well.

A copy of the play, with a note saying that I would be auditioning for the role of Darius, was sent to my dressing room at the litter-box theatre. So before I slapped on the kitty-cat makeup, I read a little and laughed. Then, while stretching before the opening, I read a little more and laughed a little more, now out loud. I found myself unable to put the script down during intermission or during my breaks offstage. It was a gay-themed AIDS comedy, and, strange as that seems, it was funny and brilliant. Just the perfect cutting-edge type of play I wanted to be associated with. I was to audition for the role of Darius, a truly innocent but typical dancer/chorus boy who was appearing in Tommy Tune's Broadway show *Grand Hotel*. A strapping brunette with severe eyebrows, I thought I was anything but a dancer/chorus boy, typical or atypical. Slight and blond I was not. In retrospect, many times I was cast in roles that for some reason or another I thought I was not properly suited for, and even more I was not cast in roles that I thought myself perfect for. This is a crazy subjective business, so I followed the great words of Phyllis Newman: go to the audition, take the job, and ask questions later.

Despite my ever-present fear of rejection, I went to the call at the casting office of Johnson, Liff, and Zerman. I had prepared the requested scenes, and wore my audition uniform of fitted black jeans, denim shirt, and black boots. For years I would tend to be so focused or nervous at auditions that I sometimes could not recall what I did or how it went, but this one was different. There was no pressure because I had a good job already, and Paul Rudnick and the director, Chris Ashley, made me feel at ease from the start. I thought it went well, and the next day Bill called to say that indeed the audition had gone very well, and that I was to be called back the next week.

Mom was scheduled to visit New York the same dates, for what she called her Bryan fix. She would come up a few times a year, at least once with Aunt Carol and Uncle Jack, who had become second parents to me since my father's death. They consistently went above and beyond the call of duty with their kindness, love, and generosity. Family is one thing, but I do believe in the family of choice. By this point Moozie was living with Mom. She had moved in after Dad died, and would stay until she died ten years later. Arrangements had been made for Moozie to stay with Aunt Vilma when Mom was traveling. Throughout this period, Moozie would be in and out of the hospital and at death's door so many times that we nicknamed her "Boomerang," because she always came back.

I met them as they were finishing getting settled in their suite at the Regency. Aunt Carol was dressed in head-to-toe polka dots with a huge hat, sporting a vibrant bunch of red cherries. Aunt Carol never held back. She was and is her own wonderful creation, and I adore that about her. Usually we would head directly to La Grenouille for lunch. Mom and Carol admired the breathtaking floral arrangements, and Uncle Jack enjoyed trying his latest Creole-meets-Borscht Belt jokes on the waiters.

But oddly enough, neither the servers nor anyone else in earshot seemed to mind his political incorrectness, maybe because he would laugh so heartily at his own jokes that it became infectious and everyone joined in. But once in a while he would cross the line and I would check my salad for spit. Today Mom had an appointment with Mr. Beau at Saks, so La Grenouille and Uncle Don Rickles would have to wait until tomorrow.

Upon arriving at Saks, Mom suggested that we have a quick snack at Café SFA, as we were a little early for her appointment. As we waited in line for a table, I asked

Mom to hear my lines for my upcoming callback. She had done this many times in the past, and it was fun to watch her "act." I had forgotten about the nature of the play completely as I became more comfortable with my life. Tom had moved in, but was still a "roommate" to my family, and by this point all of my friends in New York knew, and some in New Orleans; I never really had to tell them, they just got it, knew it, and accepted me for it. Only my mother and brother didn't officially realize what was in plain view.

Nonetheless, I handed her the pages, showed her where to start, and we were off. At first I don't think she really understood what was going on in the scene, but when I delivered something along these lines (which would later be cut), "Jeffrey, I may be HIV-positive, but I am still going to be gay, I am still going to wear my leather jacket and go dancing at the Roxy," Mom didn't flinch. She simply smiled, lowered her great tortoiseshell frames that I had picked out for her on her last visit, and said ever so softly, "Sweetheart, that was wonderful. You certainly know those lines well, and your acting was lovely, but honeydew, let's keep it down. We are in Saks."

At that moment I knew that if I landed this role, I would have to come out to her. Now I prayed to be cast, and to be cast free.

The next day we scheduled shopping and lunch around my callback, which was held at the WPA Theatre on West 23rd Street between Tenth and Eleventh avenues. My name was called, and I read the scenes to the pleasant laughter of the tiny casting audience. When I was finished, Paul Rudnick asked, laughing his inimitable laugh, "Bryan, are you *really* in *Cats*?"

I smiled, striking an iconic Gillian Lynn–choreographed cat pose, answering, "Yup, now and forever."

This cracked the room up, as the often-mocked advertising line for the show was "Cats: Now and Forever!" I did get the role, but then Paul rewrote my part to actually be a chorus boy from *Cats,* so there would be no escaping unitard and leg warmers for at least another year. *Jeffrey* opened to rave reviews and played a limited engagement at the WPA, then transferred to the Minetta Lane Theatre in the West Village for an open-ended commercial run. Mom and her entourage came north to see the critically acclaimed show, and even though I had warned her about the language and subject matter, I wasn't sure how she'd react.

She was dealing with several painful and stressful issues at the time, including selling our family home that Dad had designed and built, moving to a town house that I did not like or approve of, and dealing with Moozie's ongoing medical issues. But I had to tell her, as I had vowed in Saks. I had to bite the bullet and just do it. So, the night after she saw the show, we came back to my apartment. Tom had gone out, and after a bottle of wine, when I could no longer avoid her questions or her eyes, I told her.

It wasn't horrible; it wasn't easy. I still wonder how she didn't already know, like everyone else. I mean, I had picked out her clothes, shoes, handbags, and jewelry since sixth grade. I hadn't had a girlfriend for years. And I lived with a very handsome man in a *one-bedroom apartment! Remember Liza! Get a calculator and figure it out!*

Although there were some tears, she assured me that we all would be fine, that she loved me, I was her son, she loved Tom, and together we all would have understanding, and love. Surprisingly, when I told my "good ole boy" brother, who I feared telling the most, it was a breeze. He said disarmingly, "You're gay? Thank God, I thought you just weren't getting any!"

My fears had been a waste of time. Nothing had really changed between me and my mother and brother, but finally the truth had been told.

But I know it wasn't all smooth sailing for Mom. She made a very important phone call as soon as she set a Ferragamo-clad heel back in the Big Easy. I can hear her now . . .

"Oh, Dr. Sugar, this is Gayle Batt calling . . . Remember? Bryan's mother? Yes, he's fine . . . yes, he's in his second Broadway show and loving it . . . well, the *Times Picayune* is very sweet. Well, I'm . . . I'm . . . Dr. Sugar, I really need to speak with you . . ."

The Bees

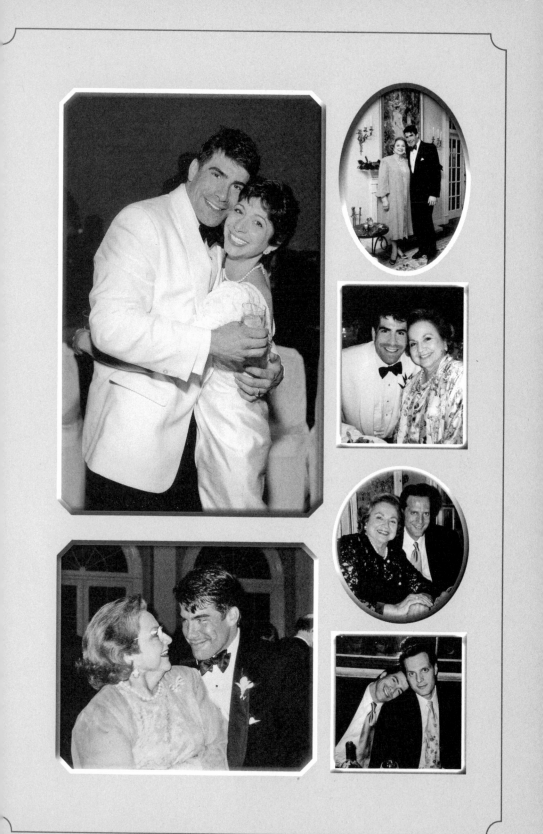

THE FIRST SYNAGOGUE I entered was Temple Beth Israel Touro on Saint Charles Avenue, just a hop, skip, and jump down the block from Moozie's home. It was seventh grade and I was there to witness my new classmate's call to the Torah. Nathaniel Kaplan was a round, squat transfer student from Uruguay whose rare pituitary disorder had unfortunately caused him to resemble Hervé Villechaize of *Fantasy Island* television fame. Some of the cooler and crueler Newman School upperclassmen would shout, "The plane, boss, the plane!" whenever he was in earshot.

Having endured the brunt of their occasional slurs upon my masculinity—or lack thereof—I felt compassion for this heavily accented, lisping South American imp, and for a short while we actually became friends. That is, until, in a heated discussion, he accused me and my comrade Leann of not being good Jews. Mistake. I replied, "That would be correct on only one count, Nate, since I'm not a Jew. I'm a Protestant. But Leann is a Jew and a damn good one at that!"

Leo, as she was recently nicknamed, explained that Nathaniel was Orthodox and she was Reformed, and there was a big difference. I didn't know there were different kinds of Jews, nor did it matter to me. I had Jewish friends whose families actually put up Christmas trees, and didn't even bother to call them "Hanukkah bushes." I loved the rare exotic foods Leo's mother, Miss Lillian, served. She was known citywide for her pickled herring, chopped liver, and latkes, all with a spicy Southern Creole twist, naturally. Such ethnic cuisine was only available to me from Miss Lillian's fabulous kitchen. None of it, not even a bagel, much less lox, would ever have been served at my home.

Despite this minor altercation, Leo and I and the rest of our middle-school class were invited to Nathaniel's bar mitzvah celebration. Although some of the more narrow-minded parents did not allow their Gentile young to attend, I happily went with a sense of pride and adventure at the possible opportunity to say *mazel tov*.

Recently confirmed myself, I had not the slightest desire to invite anyone from my crisp Izod-clad uptown school to my polyester blue-collar Irish channel church, not even Leann. At that time, and, I believe, still today, there is a great chasm in New Orleans society dictated by what you wear, where you live, how you speak, and, most important, where you go to school, and I don't mean college. And, even though I felt a lagniappe-sized portion of guilt, I decided it was best not to mix school and state, as it were. I was just now coming to terms with all kinds of prejudice, racial, religious, and socioeconomic. It was everywhere, and I was a naïve and sheltered kid who believed what he was taught in Sunday school.

There was no such guilt or narrow-mindedness in my classmates by the time of my second visit to a synagogue, Temple Sinai, also on Saint Charles Avenue, twenty years later. And this time I wasn't just a spectator at the festivities; I would be a groomsman and usher to Miss Lillian at Leann's wedding.

At my mother's new town house in Old Metairie, a suburb nestled in the the crescent city of New Orleans, I had showered and shaved hastily, donned my white dinner jacket and tux, and raced to the temple for pre-wedding photos. Tom remained at home and would escort Mom to the nuptials later that evening.

Tom has a knack for experiencing Mom during some of her finest moments. We've entertained many a cocktail or dinner party on his stories for years, such as the one about the time during our stay two years previously, when Tom realized that he had omitted shampoo while packing our more than ample supply of sundries and colognes, and ventured down the hallway to ask Mom if he could borrow hers.

"Oh dawlin', I don't wash my own hair," she answered, giggling.

This evening would be no different. Tom realized that he had once again forgotten to bring an essential tool, hairspray, which he was confident Mom possessed in abundance. So once again he made his way to her door and knocked gently, saying, "Gayle, I hate to disturb you while you're getting ready, but do you have any hairspray I could borrow? I seem to have forgotten ours in New York."

According to Tom, Mother opened one of the French doors and showed her honey-colored coif and perfectly painted face. She struggled to just reveal her face and to hide the rest of her ample figure behind the narrow door.

"Oh dawlin', thank goodness you knocked. Now I know you've seen your mother in her slip, so could you please be an angel and help me? I can't seem to get my dress over my hair."

Tom entered the lacy, feminine bedroom area with apprehension and trepidation similar to that of a bad scene in a lesser Tennessee Williams play. Mom held out the subtle pink floral silk dress and draping chiffon kimono ensemble designed and hand-painted for her by her dear friend Ray Cole, a noted local designer and artist.

"Now, sweetie, if you could just help me guide the shift over my hair. Skip, the living doll who usually does my hair, is out of town, so Miss Rhonda was the only one available at the salon, and she does my hair all right I guess, it's not like Skip, no one is. Do you think it's too big? Too high? Does it look like a blondish helmet? Be honest, lamb, maybe we could tone it down, have you ever done your mother's hair?"

Tom delicately helped the slippery fabric over the "do," much to Mom's delight.

"There, Gayle, you look great, the hair is perfect, not too big, not too small, just right. And no, I can't say that

I've done my mother's hair before . . . unless dyeing it counts."

They shared a chuckle as he retrieved the desired hair-spray and headed for the door while Mom bustled about the room, donning the sheer kimono and fiddling with diamond and pearl earbobs.

"Oh, Tommy, I hate like the dickens to ask, but would you be a dear and pour us a glass of wine? I'd do it my-self, but my knees are so bad that I can't maneuver the stairs anymore, and the elevator takes so darn long I'm afraid we'd be late to the wedding, and we've got to have a good seat. It's the Kendall Jackson Chardonnay in the fridge. Now, on the other hand, if you'd rather a martini, I know how you gentlemen love your Ketel One martinis, I wouldn't be contrary to that notion myself."

"Two martinis, then. Cold, and dry with a twist all right?"

"You are from heaven above, you simply are."

Hauling out her jewelry from various secret hiding places throughout her boudoir, Mom tried to move faster than her legs or body would allow, a practice that sadly often resulted in a fall. While she clasped a single strand of South Sea pearls in her right hand, and a double strand of opera-length nine millimeter in her left, Tom reentered the chamber with the drinks poised on a small silver tray.

"You are too much, Tom, you are. This is fit for a queen. I never use the silver anymore, but that's what it's there for, to be enjoyed. That's what Bryanny-boy says all the time. Dawlin', *merci beaucoup*!"

Pearls still in hand, she picked up the cocktail, spilling

a tiny drop from the perfect pour, eliciting her stock response for such occasions, "Well, honey, that's the wonderful thing about martinis, whatever you spill makes a great astringent. Tom, which do you think, South Sea or double-strand opera?"

"I'd go with the double-strand opera."

"But I love the South Seas so much, and everyone has seen these before."

"Then go with the South Seas."

"Thank you, I will. Sweetheart, you have been such a great help, could I trouble you for one more thing? Would you be so kind as to help me pin on my bees?"

Bees? thought Tom.

Ceremoniously, Mom revealed two of her most prized possessions: a pair of pavé diamond bee pins. Their sentimental value was far greater than their monetary worth. They were the last gift my father had given her before he died. She gently placed the gem-encrusted insects in Tom's hand.

Mother and Tom, the bearer of the bees, positioned themselves at her makeup table, he behind her, both gazing into the ornate gilded mirror. With each attempt to attach the bees to the delicate silk dress, the sheer weight of the brooches caused them to fall, pulling the fine material down with them, dangling, unnatural, and unattractive. After a few unsuccessful tries, Mom softly suggested, "Dawlin', honey, you have to go under the bra strap and attach the bees to the shoulder pad. I do believe that's the only way these critters will stay on this flimsy silk."

At this moment, Tom's only thought besides *Dear God,*

let this moment pass quickly, was *Bryan owes me sooooo big for this!*

Finally, Tom was able to position the bees so that they perched looking outward from each other on her shoulder. As they both stared in the mirror, Mother tilted her dainty head and gestured expressively with her hands as she said, "Oh, Tom, honey. Now I appreciate how you have the bees all aloof like that, but Bryan prefers when the bees are talking to each other!"

The cold, hard fact was that I truly didn't care how communicative the bees were. This, of course, was her diplomatic way of saying, "No, dawlin', that's not it, try again." Tom took a few more sips of his martini, placed the brooches to Mother's liking, and at last all was well in her world. After a few more hours of primping, they hopped in a cab, as I had taken the car.

"Oh, driver," she lilted, "would you mind rolling up the windows and giving that air conditioning a big boost, after all it is a hundred degrees outside, and the wind will muss my hair, thank you kindly."

As they drove down Metairie Road, Mom pointed out the historic cemetery where her daddy and my father were buried. Then she stopped and leaned forward. "Oh, driver, would you be a dear and turn down the volume on the radio, and while you're there please change the station to Bayou 107, WBYU, I believe those are the call letters, they play such relaxing music, don't you agree?"

"Sure thing, Mrs. Batt. Maybe you don't remember me, but I used to work at the Beach, the Zephyr rollercoaster. It's me, Li'l Ant'ny," he replied.

"Well, I declare! Little Anthony, you also worked at the Bali Hai Restaurant . . . yes? Isn't that something, after all these years. Well, no wonder I didn't recognize you, sweetheart. The only time I rode the Zephyr, they had to drag me on and then carry me off!"

They both laughed and shared memories of New Orleans' beloved Pontchartrain Beach. Soon they arrived at the entrance to the temple, and as Tom escorted her while she hurriedly slipped on her white gloves, she whispered softly, "You know something, dear, I don't think that I've ever been inside this temple before, all these years, now isn't that something?"

Tom replied, "Oh, that's something, all right."

The wedding was splendid beyond compare. I teared up as I always do. I actually enjoy the occasional cry, and especially at weddings of those I love. Leann and I had been fast and solid friends since nursery school. It's a remarkable bond that I cherish.

The breathtaking houppa was figured from vibrant magnolia and legustrum boughs masterfully intertwined with palm fronds and dozens upon dozens of assorted white lilies, roses, and gardenia. The groomsmen sported dashing white dinner jackets; I've always loved their James Bond appeal. And since it was the Friday prior to Labor Day, Leann decided that rather than torture her bridesmaids with hideously hued dresses, her attendants would all wear white dresses in a style of their choosing— subject to her discerning approval. All of our high school friends looked stunning.

Soon after the ceremonial glass was smashed, and the

newlyweds kissed, we were rushed to our limousines and whisked with police escort downtown to the Fairmont Hotel, which Mother archaically still refers to as the Roosevelt. A sumptuous cocktail hour ensued while photographers snapped countless candid shots and posed the reluctant crew for even more. Miss Lillian was beaming, but constantly made sure that no one had a drink in hand in any of the formal shots.

Suddenly, from the back of the crowded room, the Olympia Brass Jazz Band started to play the second line. Usually I shy away from New Orleans traditions like the second line as common and hackneyed. The idea of dancing behind a jazz band while twirling an umbrella or handkerchief seems so forced and unnatural to me. Tonight, however, I was completely caught up in the euphoria; I twirled my handkerchief with sheer abandon as we made our way into the lavish grand ballroom.

The food was amazing, pirogue boats brimming with iced oysters on the half shell, shrimp with rémoulade sauces, salmon, and various caviars. There were delicious hors d'oeuvres of every variety, and skirted floral festooned stations serving a multitude of perfectly prepared baby lamb chops, medallions of rosemary pork tenderloin, and peppercorn-encrusted filet mignon. There was too much to recall or describe. Such a wedding feast I'd never seen before.

Rockin' Dopsie, a famed local zydeco-soul-funk band, started to wail, and the dance floor was instantly packed with couples of all ages gyrating to the hypnotic sound. Toward the middle of the evening they announced the

Horah, and mispronounced some of the Hebrew lyrics. I do believe that in one of the verses I actually heard "Have a tequila" instead of "Hava Nagila." Fortunately, both Tom and I had been involved with productions of *Fiddler on the Roof,* and were familiar with the dance steps and basically when to lift the bride and groom on their chairs during the climax. Some onlookers, mainly those who hadn't attended the bar mitzvahs years ago, stared in bewilderment at the pageantry. Personally, I adore and relish other cultures' ceremonies and traditions, even the questionably mercenary Cajun money dance, in which, while dancing with the bride, cold, hard cash is proudly pinned onto her veil.

After hours of merriment, Leann and Teddy bowed and exited the gala, our cue to leave as well. But never wanting the party to end, my dear friend Leslie and her soon-to-be fiancé, Bryan (spelled just like my own name), decided that we should venture into the French Quarter and make a pilgrimage to Pat O'Brien's famous yet touristy bar to have our photo taken next to the flaming courtyard fountain in order to preserve the night. I made sure Mom had a ride home, and then Tom and I set out with them.

We crossed the once-beautiful Canal Street, which used to be home to wonderful locally owned department stores such as D. H. Holmes, Godchaux's, and Gus Mayer. Now they are just a memory, owing to the exodus of retailers from downtown and the area's subsequent decline. Elegant storefronts were now replaced by T-shirt merchants, athletic shoe shops, and check-cashing joints. Nevertheless, inebriated, we made our way to Bourbon Street, passing through the crowds of raucous, Mardi Gras–beaded tourists carrying go-cups filled with various alcoholic concoctions.

Although we most definitely did not blend into the raucous, mismatched crowd, no one among the throngs seemed to notice or care. As we passed the Old Absinthe House Bar, a stumbling, tank-topped queen twirled into my path and, laying his hand on my chest, cried sadly in a thick New Orleans–Brooklynese accent, "Oh my Gawd, baby, did ya hear? Princess Di's been in a bad, bad car wreck, and they think she's dead!"

One of his comrades pulled him away, but moving deeper into the fray, we heard his pitiful cries over the din. "Oh my Gawd, I loved her . . . I loved her!"

In an intoxicated haze of disbelief, we continued on to the famed patio. We'd mourn the tragic death of the princess tomorrow. Now was a time to celebrate love and life and friendship. We raised our glasses again and again, willfully drowning anything else but celebration.

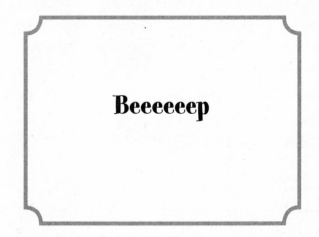

Beeeeeep

"Hello, anybody home? Yoo-hoo! I guess not. Well anyhoo, sweetie pie, how's my favorite little Broadway actor doing? I need your help if you don't mind, I am swamped. On the fifteenth—or is it the sixteenth?—now hold your horses, it can't be the sixteenth because that's the Mad Hatter's Luncheon for the Opera Guild. Oh, that reminds me. If you happen to be in Saks or Bergdorf's and see a fabulous fun hat, you know how they do at the Mad Hatter's Luncheon—wait a second, have you gone? Maybe that was Jay. No, I think it was you when you were in college and modeled for Saks down here, or was it Rubenstein Brothers? No, it was the Men of Fashion I'm thinking of . . . Where was I? . . . Hat? . . . Oh, hell's bells I'm having a senior moment, I Sewanee, I think I'm getting 'old timer's disease' like Oralea. Oh puddin', she's not well at all, not at all, she can't remember a thing. Now I know I wanted to tell you something and it was no story . . . something about . . . got it . . . Please, pretty please, on your way to the theatre would you, as soon as possible, stop by the Feragamo boutique on Fifth Avenue, I think they're having a sale, but that's neither here nor there. I'm desperate. Saks down here doesn't have any of the 'tuxedo' pumps like I wear, you know, the ones with the bows on the front. Well, can you believe they're out of my size in bone and black patent? I'm ashamed to admit my foot has actually grown, even though I've lost ten pounds, aren't you proud? Anyhoo I now wear size ten, and to add insult to injury, the width is now wide, I could just cry, but I've bigger fish to fry, can't worry about that today, I'll worry about that tomorrow. Just ask for Vincent. He's a dear, he knows me, and it's bone and black patent and have him send them overnight. I'll save the tax, but the shipping always gets ya in the end. There's something else that I . . . oh yes, if you happen to be in Saks in the next couple of days, or you could stop by after you go to Feragamo, see Beau. You know Mr. Beau. He's an angel. I need a smart daytimey suit 'cause I'm getting honored at the Cancer Crusaders' Tea, I trust your taste implicitly, and an evening . . . but I don't think they're wearing long to the Art in Bloom Ball at the museum anymore, are they? I'll check because then I could wear one of Ray Cole's dresses to Art in Bloom, they're exquisitely hand-painted silk and look really artsy, don't you think? You know Ray. What am I thinking? But, honey, if you're in the fashion district, I know that's just a hop, skip, and a jump from your theatre, please stop by that beautiful fabric shop, I think it's called B and J. I am walking on air about Jay and Andree's engagement, aren't you, Mister best man? How's about them apples, I can remember that name because the initials stand for my two favorite sons. I only have you two, Bryan and Jay, B. and J. Anyhoo, if you see any of their beautiful floral silks, you know, the prints that look soft and feminine like a Monet or Renoir, you know what we like, I need five yards. But the most important thing, first thing on the list is the pumps. Thank you sooooo much. I love you hawd, hawd, hawd swear to Gawd. Oh, by the way, it's Mother."

Beeeeeep!

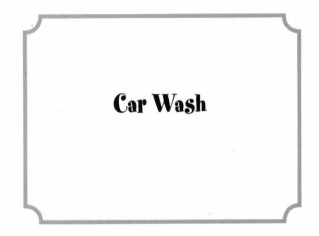

Car Wash

"UNCLE MYRON, ARE YOU UP?" It was my childhood and lifelong pal Chuck Menendez, who now, although a respected married physician and father of four, still calls me Uncle Myron due to our own "-yron" language we created at six years old and have perpetuated to the present.

"Chyron, what's up?" I answered, a bit groggy as I awakened with a mild martini hangover. I never kept a phone in the bedroom, but last night was an exception. Mom was visiting New York to see me as Lumiere, the singing and dancing French candelabra in Disney's *Beauty and the Beast,* and we had early-morning plans to rent a car and drive to the Woodbury Commons deluxe designer outlet mall for a crisp September day of high-end bargain hunting. We could rent a wheelchair there if her hip and/or knee got tired or ached, so we were all set. Tom stirred and made his way to our recently remodeled postage-stamp-sized kitchen, where he could amazingly produce gourmet dinners for twelve, but making coffee was his sole purpose this morning.

"Turn on NBC or any station; I think a plane hit the World Trade Center," Chuck said.

"Oh, that's awful," I said into the receiver and, flipping on the TV, then, "Tom, come in and see this, a plane hit the Trade Center, do they know anything?"

"They think it was a small commuter plane, but that's so weird," Chuck replied.

"I know, are the people getting out? It's early yet, let's hope not too many are at work . . . OH MY GOD!"

"HOLY SHIT, NO!"

"OH GOD, NO!"

The second plane had hit, and Tom and I stood in utter shock and disbelief. The newscasters mentioned the possibility of a terrorist attack. Staring at the screen in fear, we prayed and hoped that people could get out of the buildings, never dreaming the horrible sight we'd witness next: figures jumping from windows, people suffering a horrific death before our eyes, and the nation's, and the world's.

"Chy, I gotta go, Mom's up here visiting, oh my God this is horrible, give my love to Margaret and the kids."

"Buddy, be careful, if you need anything, just call."

We started to make frantic calls to family and friends, making sure everyone was all right. In New York, especially in the theatre, your friends become your family. Then the towers went down, and as they fell I crumpled to the ground, screaming. Tom's big, beautiful eyes were glued to the Sony in complete disbelief. A second or two passed, and he quickly pulled me to my feet. Calmly he said, "Call your

mom at the DoubleTree Suites. Times Square could be a target. I'm going to get water and canned goods, and I should
call Leslie and get milk and food for her and the baby."

Mom usually stayed closer to me, but since she walked
with the aid of a cane and was having severe orthopedic
challenges, I took advantage of my Broadway connections
and discounts to get her a suite right across Broadway
from the Lunt-Fontanne Theatre, in the heart of the theatre district. Nothing was going to stop her from seeing
me in one of my Broadway shows—never had in the past,
and never would.

"Mom, have you seen the TV, do you know what's
going on?" I said, with panic creeping into my voice, "Get
in a cab and get to my place now. You know the address,
just make sure the driver goes east and up, or through the
park if it's open—just not near anything some nut would
want to blow up. What am I saying? That's all of fucking
New York!" Obviously, the gravity of the situation had
not registered.

"Bryan, my pet, you know I can't hear you when you
use that kind of language."

"Mother, do you know what's going on? You are in the
Times Square area, it's a target. Get in a cab and get here
NOW!"

"Okay baby dear, but I haven't put on my face yet."

"Mom, just take your purse—and for the love of God,
come here now!"

"All right, sweetie, calm down, I'll be there soon. Love
you, bye-bye now."

"Love you too."

Tom mentioned that if Mom could not get a cab, there would be no way for her to walk, and public transportation might be suspended, so we decided that I would rent a wheelchair at the medical supplies shop on the corner of Second Avenue and 72nd, and Tom would get food and other essentials. As I went to dress, I overheard him talking to our friend Leslie, who had just given birth. Her husband was probably safe in Midtown, but she was in a panic just like the rest of the city. Tom assured her that her husband would call as soon as he could, and in the meantime he would get milk and Pampers for our godchild Audrey.

"I'm off!" I said, running for the door, but as soon as I reached for the knob, I ran back and embraced Tom. We didn't know what was going to happen, whether our world would end before wheelchairs and milk were acquired, but right now it was not about wheelchairs and milk.

"I love you," I said. "Love you too," he replied, and then I was on the streets on one of the clearest, crispest, most beautiful blue-sky days I'd ever witnessed in Manhattan.

Running to the medical supply shop, where I'd purchased numerous knee braces for my ever-failing knees, I watched people's tortured expressions as they cried and screamed on pay phones and cell phones, either in sorrow or in relief. Within minutes most phone service, including cell phones, was dead, adding even more fear and doubt to the already dire situation. As I rented the wheelchair from a rather calm lady, I explained my situation and she informed me that the subways were not running, so the best way to get to Times Square—actually Duffy Square, as she pointed out, is the correct name of the area at 46th and 47th Street and Broadway where Mother's hotel was located—was to take the bus. But who knew how far it would go downtown?

Pushing the empty wheelchair, I walked for a couple of blocks before a bus finally came. I immediately noticed something odd: people were talking to each other. One man was listening to his radio and informing the passengers when there was an update. Then they would comment and discuss. As I struggled to find my Metro card while balancing the cumbersome chair, a pierced and punkish student came to my aid as the bus driver kindly told me that this ride was on him.

We edged our way slowly downtown from 74th Street, only to be halted a few blocks later by a police barricade stopping all traffic. Not knowing what was going on or what buildings or areas to avoid, I thought it safe to walk south and westward across town through Central Park, exiting at Seventh Avenue and Central Park South. Like a salmon swimming upstream, I made my way pushing the wheelchair through the masses marching north to escape Midtown and downtown. Finally I emerged onto Seventh Avenue, where still more people poured out against the usual traffic flow. So many people and sounds and cries and shouts overwhelmed my senses. The whole journey is a blur. Somewhere on the way, I bumped into an old friend, Marc Cherry, who would later create *Desperate Housewives,* and he joined me in case I needed extra help with Mother.

Upon arrival at the DoubleTree, I called room 1023, but there was no answer, and then the front desk informed me that Mrs. Gayle Batt had indeed checked out, and told me what a charming mother I had. Marc went back to his hotel, but gave me his cell phone number in hopes the phones would soon be receiving better service. Then I commenced the long journey back home through the sea of weary, shattered New Yorkers, once again with an empty wheelchair in tow.

I have heard some crazy things in my day, just plumb looney-tunes crazy, but on the walk home I actually heard a woman say with a thick Brooklyn accent, "This is a crying shame, that Trade Center was so nice. They just did all those beautiful renovations and everything, and them nice stores like Ann Taylor and everything. Did you ever see the gorgeous Banana Republic there? I just think it's tragic that a nice shopping mall like that . . ."

I wanted to scream and wring her insensitive neck, but of course I didn't. However, I noticed how people, with the exception of this moron, had been so kind and helpful all day, no pushing, not a foul word or ugly gesture since the towers fell. So instead of telling her off, I simply said, to her utter bewilderment, "Bellevue is to the right."

After what seemed an eternity, I wheeled the chair out of the park at the 79th Street entrance and straight along the wide thoroughfare that was my home for years. Mixed with anger, despair, and violation was an odd comfort when I saw national guardsmen with automatic rifles in front of various consulates of foreign nations. My feelings would soon turn to horror when tanks lined Fifth Avenue, and concrete barricades were placed to prevent car bombings of the local churches and synagogues.

Finally arriving at the apartment, I opened the door to see Tom and Mom with big balloon glasses of Chardonnay, one ready to be poured for me. There were frantic hugs and kisses and tears all around. Mom said sweetly, "Bryanny boy, I hope you don't mind, but I think we needed a little sip to take the edge off."

"Sip!" Tom said, laughing. "Gayle had three cases delivered."

I sat, and they filled me in about what they had heard on the news. Tom had gotten an air mattress for us to sleep on, and Mom would take our bed. Tom marveled at how great New Yorkers are, and we all toasted as he recalled his trip to the Gristede's grocery down the block. Everyone was frantically acquiring canned goods, water, and supplies, but people were actually being helpful and courteous. He was amazed that one customer actually said, "Excuse me, but I believe you were in front of me in line."

It was the first and only laugh of the day, short-lived but hearty. Luckily the few people we knew who worked in the World Trade Center were either late to work or got out in time. Mom had asked Tom and would later ask me constantly if there was anyone she should pray for, to which I could only reply, "Everyone, us included." I marveled at her faith, her unswerving faith that had seen her through and would continue to see her through more and more tragedies, illnesses, and heartbreaks. For a multitude of reasons, my faith was on hold.

"Dawlin', I've got to fix my face for dinner. I think it's

just lovely that everyone is getting together . . . Oh baby dear, we didn't tell you?"

Tom chimed in, "Everyone is going over to Rachel and Lenny's. Leslie and Bryan are bringing gumbo. We are bringing wine. Cliff and Jimmy and John and Jeff are coming, too. Dinner under distress."

Gayle added, "Tommy, my love, you sure there's no Southern blood in you? That's what we do! When things are bad and when things are good and when it's really bad, bad, bad, and it's bad, bad, bad now, we get together and eat . . . I know it's not just a Southern thing my heart, but I just think gumbo helps everything along."

These are our best friends in New York, our family; there was no way we would or could not be together this night of all nights. Of course we ran a bit behind schedule because someone couldn't find the right Ray Cole scarf to match her dinner ensemble, so Tom and I waited while Miss Prissy preened and puffed. Finally she emerged, ready to once again meet, greet, and entertain my friends, who adored her. I walked out with the wheelchair, and Mom said, "Well, I just have the two most handsome escorts; these New York ladies are going to be so jealous, I Sewanee. Dolls, I have a little problem, not big, medium size—with my bad hip and knee, I can't get into that old high bathtub of yours. Now I think it's lovely and deep, like a small swimming pool, but I just can't get in it."

I quickly thought of many possibilities—all frightening—but the most horrifying was the possibility of actually seeing Mom nude or having to bathe her. I love and adore her, but there are some things a son must never,

ever have to endure if at all possible. So quickly I thought of a solution. "Okay, Mother . . . how about I draw the bath, you put on a robe, I get a step stool and help you into the tub, then we close the shower curtain, you hand me the robe, and *voilà*!"

She countered, "Pet, I just don't see how I would get out, and it's slippery, and I'm not too steady. The last thing we need is me with a broken hip. The hospitals are busy enough with . . . oooh, that reminds me. Were the lines to donate blood shorter, because we must do that, pumpkin, we simply must."

"Mom, I don't think they need as much as they thought. It's so horrible to imagine, but there were not as many sur-vivors as we hoped." With those chilling yet true words, there came a hush over the conversation as we decided to table the bathtub discussion for now and wheeled east to Madison Avenue and my dear college friend's glamorously large flat, with a case of Kendall Jackson Chardonnay on Mom's lap.

She broke the silence. "Petunia, we should stop and get some flowers. I just love that you can pass these en-tire sweet little corner groceries and they have the most beautiful bouquets, that's what we need to bring too. Now what blossoms should we get? Tommy dear, what's your expert opinion?"

Tom and I shared a glance; she was on tonight, clearly diffusing and entertaining, but it was just the start. "Gayle, why not sunflowers? It's fall and there should be sunflowers at every bodega on the East Side."

"I knew you'd know. That's perfect, Tom. Let me tell

you something. That Tom, he's the go-to guy when you need something done right or the perfect suggestion. I'll never forget those gorgeous arrangements you did for that beautiful seventieth birthday party you and Bryanny, Jay and Andree gave me at Le Petit Theatre. That just meant so much to me to have it at that beautiful historic theatre I love so much, and the invitation was breathtaking, everyone marveled. Tom, I must ask you a big favor. Aunt Carol is turning seventy next year, and I would love to do a dinner party at the club. Would you mind helping with the invitations? Nobody has such imaginative and fun ideas as you, pet. Now Bryanny boy, what flowers do you think we should get tonight?"

There was a beat, then laughter, and she quickly added, "Well, of course sunflowers. I was just checking to see if you agreed, but sunflowers are so happy and that's what we need indeed—some happy. Oh, Tommy, I hope I didn't hurt your feelings. It's just my way, I guess, for some reason I just have to ask everyone's opinion, drives that son of mine crazy."

"Try all three of us: me, Jay, and Tom. Mom, it only drives me crazy because you know damn well what you want, and how to get it, but you still play this little game of getting everyone's approval. It kind of diffuses the value of our opinions."

"Okey-dokey, lamb chop, I hear you loud and clear. That is going at the top of the list of self-improvements," she agreed.

We arrived at Rachel's with wine, a huge bouquet of sunflowers, and a wheelchair. In the show *Beauty and the*

Beast, I carried on both hands heavy pyrotechnic-capable candlesticks as part of my elaborate costume, and due to the eight performances per week, my arms were usually exhausted. I thought they were tired from pushing an empty wheelchair for miles and miles through the streets of Manhattan, but that was nothing compared to the strain of the added weight of Mom and a case of vino up Carnegie Hill. Lumiere was beat.

Everyone was there, candles were lit, food was being prepared, and the table was being set. It felt almost like an impromptu Thanksgiving dinner. And in a way it was. We had not yet learned, nor would we learn, of any close friends who were missing. Though my heart was broken by the day's events, there was comfort in the communing. I think we all felt it. We did not know what the future held, or if there would even be one, but we were together this night.

"Rachel, dawlin'," Mom said, beaming, "you look lovely as ever, and your home is just so roomy and chic, give me a hug, sweetie, and where's your handsome lucky husband?"

She hugged Mom like she was a relative. She adored my mother and father, and while we were at Tulane together, she would drive out to our lakefront home just to watch TV with my dad or chat with Mom, even without me there.

"Oh, Mrs. Batt, we are so happy you are here. Lenny went to get some ice; he'll be right back."

"Angel, I am just going to cry if you don't call me Aunt Gayle, or Gayle. 'Mrs. Batt' is so 1985." With that, Mom cracked herself up, and her gentle laughter reminded Rachel that we were family.

"Yes, ma'am," Rachel replied, to which Mom pouted and raised an eyebrow.

"Yes, Aunt Gayle."

"That's more like it, puddin'. Now let's get me out of this contraption before people think I'm as old as I feel. I don't mind feeling old, just don't love looking old!"

Cliff and Jimmy and John and Jeff came in the room, drinks in hand. They knew Tom and I would need a double Ketel and soda with lemon, and it was made and waiting. We hugged our dear friends, and soon the entire home was a buzz of hugging, stories of the day's events, and friends to add to Mom's prayer list.

Just then the door opened. It was another dear friend, Leslie, carrying baby Audrey, and her husband, Bryan, carrying the gumbo. She announced in her best Cajun accent, "Okay, y'all, da gumbo is here, *cher*!"

Mom clamored, "Where is that gorgeous baby, let me see that beautiful girl . . . of course you too, Leslie heart, and Mr. Bryan . . . Oh she's a dream, those eyes, what an angel!"

Now the focus was on the baby and cooing, more kisses, more drinks, and stories of the day.

Soon the whole apartment was filled with the hearty aroma of Leslie's gumbo and Rachel's red beans and rice, both Louisiana girls who know Creole comfort food.

Mom spent the evening charming and disarming everyone's fears as she told stories of living through World War II. She and baby Audrey were the perfect diversion from the tragic events of the day, and although everyone still was in shock, this familial convergence helped ease the steely tension and pain, if only for a few moments at a time. Rachel had turned off the TV, there was no new news, just more sensational graphics, more fear, sadness, and shock. And soon it was time to make the pilgrimage home. Completely exhausted, Tom and I wheeled Mom back to our place, and while we got ready for bed, she made phone calls to friends and family. I overheard just a bit.

"Oh, Vilma, everyone was so nice. All of Bryan's and Tom's sweet friends got together and made gumbo and red beans and rice . . . and we are going to everyone's home for the next few days for dinner. Honestly, everyone is shaken up, scared to death, but what can we do really, it's all in hands of the man upstairs. No, they canceled all the Broadway shows, but I believe that Thursday Bryan has to go back to work. Yes, Thursday, well, we must get back to normal, whatever that is. Tell everyone that we are fine and I'll be home as soon as I can . . . I am . . . I am so glad to be here right now, I'd be worried sick if I weren't, believe it or not, and call me crazy, I'm actually happy that I am in New York right now. Love you too. Bye."

"Baby dear," she called, "I have been trying to get Delta on the phone to change my ticket. I'm supposed to fly out Thursday, but no one is answering the phone."

"Mom, you are not going anywhere, not for a while, not until the airports are up and running, and then I would like you to give it a few days, just to make sure," I answered.

"Oh, but pumpkin, I can't stay that long, I appreciate you both being so sweet, but I've got to get back, and I don't want to be a burden."

"Mom, you're not a burden, and I am not letting you get on a plane until it's safe, and that is final."

"Okay, sweetie, but, well, honey, what are we going to do about the bathtub situation, I can't get in that tub, and I noticed Rachel's is the same. While I visited the ladies' room I tried to get in her tub, but then I thought, 'Don't do that, Gayle, what if you can't get out?' That would be a fine kettle of fish. But sugar pie, I can't just take little French baths for a week. There must be a spa of sort nearby. They may have treatments or something that could work."

If I'd rolled my eyes anymore, they would have popped out of my head. "Mom, we'll deal with that tomorrow. I'm about to drop, it's been a grueling day, let's get some sleep, hmm?"

She agreed. "That's right, tomorrow is another day, Scarlett."

And with that, she ambled into the bedroom while Tom and I arranged the makeshift combination air mattress and pillow bed on our living room floor, somehow knowing that despite our fatigue, no sleep would come. Goodnight kisses and hugs were dispensed, and the light was left on in the bathroom as a night-light for all. I realized then that I was very much like her, that if there was something I wanted or needed, no matter how foolish or nonsensical, I wouldn't rest until it was mine.

In the middle of the night, after awaking from a short and light slumber, I overheard a voice coming from the bedroom, so I made my way to the door, only to hear, "Yes, is this Delta Airlines? Oh good, this is Gayle Batt and I am scheduled to fly from New York to New Orleans this . . . Oh, there's not . . . Well, do you know when service will be returning . . . Uh-huh, well, I just wanted to make sure that my ticket would be honored even though . . . um-hmm . . . I see, I understand, but you see, I was visiting my son Bryan, he plays Lumiere in *Beauty and the Beast* on Broadway . . . Oh yes, very proud and . . . what's that? . . . Oh yes, I am staying with him and his partner now . . . Oh yes, he's been in quite a few shows, *Cats* . . . me too, I loved that one, and let's see, he was in *Sunset Boulevard* and *Starlight Express* . . . Yes, that one was on roller skates, he had a terrible knee injury from that one, you know I have to go back into the body shop myself for a hip replacement, that's why I need wheelchair help at the airport. Oh, he was a dear today, he ran out and rented a wheelchair while Tom got food and water and milk for their friend's newborn baby . . . who is a little dream . . . little Audrey . . . Isn't it a pretty name, I love those old-fashioned names myself . . . No, just my two boys, I wanted a little girl but the good Lord saw fit that I have two sons and that is just fine by me . . . Beg your pardon . . . Oh yes, dear . . . blessings . . ."

"Mom, it's three a.m., what are you doing?"

She placed her hand over the receiver so the Delta representative couldn't hear. "Coach, I am just checking on my flight status, and you are right, there is no service as yet." She then went back to the agent on the phone.

"Well, you have been so sweet, darlin', what's your name? Wanda? Oh, Shwanda, that's a lovely name . . . for your uncle Sherman and aunt Wanda. What a coincidence, my godchild's name is Donna-Gayle for my brother Donald and little ol' me . . . I love interesting names . . . Well, thank you so much, Shwanda, you have a great night, day, morning . . . yes, bless you too."

THE NEXT MORNING Mom appeared in her housecoat, peering into the living room.

"Hey, you handsome boys, I didn't want to wake you, but can a gal get a cup of coffee in this four-star hotel?"

Tom answered, "Sure, Gayle, a pot is brewing. Black, right?"

"That's it on the nose. So what do we have on the docket for today? You know I am going to have to find a place that can do my hair; I think there is just a day left with this do. Honey, do you know of a nice salon that does a nice shampoo set and comb out? Oh, and by the way, did you happen to think of a spa nearby, that is a must."

"Mom, I haven't had my coffee yet. Can we just turn on the TV and see if the world still exists?"

"By all means, let's have some coffee and I'll treat to breakfast. Would you call that cute diner around the corner that delivers? I'll have eggs sunny side up with bacon, and wheat toast. My, I haven't had eggs sunny side up in ages. Baby dear, you just order whatever you'd like. Tommy, what would you like for breakfast? Waffles, pancakes, omelettes, I just love New York, the fact that you can call and order breakfast and it comes to your door still hot—well, it's amazing."

I love her, and maybe it was due to the life-altering traumatic stress we were all under and our different coping mechanisms, but on day two, I didn't know how much more I could take.

After we had a great Green Kitchen breakfast, I quickly threw on my jeans and went for a short walk while Tom showered and Gayle applied her daily war paint, a process that usually took at least forty-five minutes. The winds had changed, and uptown we could now smell just a hint of what was unbearable at the other end of the island. I just needed to move, to gather my thoughts, to find a salon to coif honey-colored cotton-candy hair into a Rams football helmet, and a spa to hose down my mother. Luckily, on the Upper East Side of Manhattan, a number of "set and comb out" ladies' beauty salons remained, and as soon as I crossed Second Avenue, I recalled a new day spa that had opened. So I walked a few blocks down, all the while trying not to let the tainted air and the fear bring me to my knees.

Upon entering the Zen-wannabe spa, I must admit I was calmed for a moment, but soon the trickling sounds of water, mixed with Zamfir-like pan-flute tunes, just agitated my stressed state of mind. Finally an employee came to my aid and asked how she might be of service.

"I never thought I would actually ever say these words to another human being, but to be honest, I need someone to bathe my mother."

I explained the bad hip and knee, the old high-lipped

bathtubs of prewar apartments, and this sweet lady actually informed me that there were many treatments in which clients were offered a finishing cleanse-rinse with mineral water and rose petals.

"Fantastic! Her name is Gayle Batt, she'll be calling soon, have fun." I quickly made my way back home. Within minutes I was wheeling her to the spa for a ginger-salt scrub and invigorating mineral and rose-petal rinse, and after that she was scheduled for a hair appointment.

About an hour and a half later, Tom and I retrieved Mother from her "treatment." We found her chatting away with the attendants. "Well, yes, if they give us comps to the show, I will bring them by, oh, here are my son and Tom now. Bryan and Tom, I'd like you to meet Norika, Soon-lin, and Tammy."

The kimono-clad ladies nodded and smiled and wished us well as they confirmed Mom's appointment for the next day. As we wheeled to the next beautification station, Mom was a wealth of conversation.

"Sweetheart, if your producers offer any free seats or discounts, I would love to give those girls tickets to see your show. They have never seen a Broadway show, and I know they would adore *Beauty*. Now, Tammy is from Queens, but the other two are from Japan, I asked them if they knew how to perform the tea ceremony. Remember when Daddy and I went to Japan and when we came home I did the tea ceremony for your class?"

Tom, in disbelief, said, "Wait a minute, Gayle, you did the tea ceremony?"

"Oh yes, she did," I replied. "For my whole second-grade

class. My teacher, Mrs. Dart, never forgot it, or my psychedelic painting of Mount Fuji."

A slight sadness came over her as she shook her head. "I don't know what happened to me. I used to be able to do so much, and I think after your daddy passed, I just kind of stopped."

"Stopped! Stopped what? I've never seen anyone do more than you, missy."

Tom added, "My God, Gayle, you've got so much going on, it makes me dizzy."

The conversation drifted back to the spa as we neared the hair salon. Tom had wanted to know just what a ginger-salt rub was, and what a rose-petal rinse was like. "Actually, Tommy dear, it's an invigorating mineral and rose-petal rinse," she said with a giggle. "Well, to start, they rub you all over with this exfoliating ginger-scented salt, and then there is a massage, and then there's this kind of, oh, I don't know what you'd call it, a sort of wheel thing that comes down and passes over you a few times. Then from all sides a gentle spray of rose water mists and mists and mists. Then they dry you and apply a protective moisturizer."

"Like a car wash?" he asked.

"Yes, sunshine, just like a car wash!"

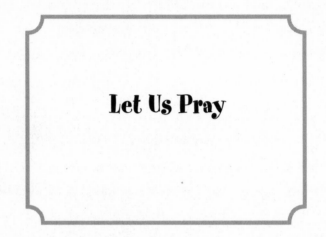

Let Us Pray

Returning to a devastated yet still beloved New Orleans just seven weeks after Katrina, Gayle was weary, but not broken. She knew she had to be strong for her family. Vilma's Broadmoor home, their childhood home, had been flooded. Uncle Donny and Aunt Irene's Uptown home was also flooded. My cousin Donna-Gayle's home in the east was washed away. Like the entire city, seventy-five percent of Mom's family's homes were flooded. But worst of all, Jay and Andrée's Lakeview home had been inundated with eight feet of standing toxic stew that completely defiled the once lush, green neighborhood. The area now looked and smelled like death. Miraculously, Mom's town house and my carriage house were virtually untouched. At first, many who resided on higher ground and sustained little or no damage to their homes expressed what was called "Katrina guilt" because they had been spared. I've never really bought into guilt, by any name. It's a useless emotion, unless you've actually done something wrong.

But as time went on, this regional sentiment waned, and the dry "Sliver by the River" was soon being called "the Isle of Denial."

We returned to a city with practically no services and amenities. Sheets of plywood still covered the shops on Magazine Street and homes' windows all over. The neutral grounds were strewn with rotten debris and rancid refrigerators. Anything that the waters touched or the creeping mold infected had to go. In Lakeview, on the great promenade of West End Avenue, there were massive three-story mountains of the discarded fabric of decimated lives— not just furniture, drapes, and rugs, but everything that forms a home and a life, the very fiber of memory. These monoliths of despair stretched for what seemed like miles. And this was just one area. Throughout the city, muddied lines, like dirty bathtub rings, covered everything in sight, marking how high the vicious waters had raged.

Restoring normalcy was impossible, for nothing ever was nor ever will be considered normal about our city or her unique children ever again. Progress, as usual, advanced at a snail's pace, but little by little services came back, groups formed to aid with the clean-up, and Americans came from everywhere to help, as our "leaders" fumbled and passed blame. Those in the community who could do so rallied and did all in their power to assist with what continues to be the arduous process of rebuilding.

We opened Hazelnut as soon as we could, not knowing if there ever would be a need now for a home-accessories and fine gift shop. We soon learned there was. Even during tragedies, wars, and every kind of disaster, people still have birthdays and get married, and Christmas arrives on December 25th just the same.

We organized Magazine Street Retail Relief, complete with wine and Bobby McIntyre's Dixieland jazz ensemble The Last Straws, to encourage other businesses to open, and stimulate commerce. Bobby returned home days early from evacuation, with drum set and straw boater in tow, so that he could "be in that number." The crestfallen yet buoyant returnees came in droves, embracing friends and family they hadn't seen since the storm, telling their stories. They were smiling, crying, laughing, sharing, and, as New Orleanians always somehow find a way to do, celebrating. Celebrating life and death, joy and pain, survival and fear. In New Orleans, all emotions are embraced with a celebration, a dance, a parade. Between fundraisers and benefits for every charity and organization imaginable, I proudly worked in Hazelnut alongside Tom and Katy, our manager, friend, confidante, and recent evacuation sister.

The newspapers and the media were vigilant about covering the enormous tragedy, but so many stories were left untold or deemed not newsworthy. So often we were given, and accepted, sensationalism disguised as "the news." Just one or two stories of the numerous heroes would have eased some pain, not much but some.

As we neared the holiday season, our shop became a bustling hub. Occasionally we served wine at sundown, but even without the grape, a pub sensibility reigned. Anytime we were behind the counter or register, people found it easy to tell their tales of loss, evacuation, and returning home—or of their hopes of returning home.

Family by family, friend by friend, everyone's road home was different, all fraught with anxiety, pathos, and miraculous glimmers of humor. Aunt Vilma's journey was particularly difficult, having to evacuate to Paula's home in Tuscaloosa, Alabama, while in the middle of heavy-duty chemotherapy for a recurrence of lung cancer. After years of smoking, the tumors had returned and a frail yet vigilant soul pressed on. Mother and she wanted to do something special for all of the family at Christmas. A needed healing.

Traditionally, from birth until I flew the coop, on Christmas Eve we all congregated at Moozie's, complete with Santa and a multitude of gifts. As she aged, we took turns decorating her signature tree with white doves and the pinkish mauve satin balls that coordinated perfectly with her defining décor hue of dusty rose. Since her death and for years prior to it, as her children's families grew, other holiday traditions emerged, but it wasn't the same, so different from the rich, inclusive familial traditions she had created.

Whenever I would see my cousins on trips home for the holidays, we all would recall sentimentally how magical those holidays had been for us as children, and wish they could be re-created. Jay would remind us of the day that he realized that Santa was Mr. Gerhardt from Pontchartrain Beach. The missing thumb, knuckle tattoo, stench of cheap bourbon, and a voice that rivaled Harvey Fierstein's might have given him away instantly, but Jay was too shocked to put the pieces together immediately. Moments before, Donna's brother Ricky had told him Santa was a capitalist myth perpetrated by the establishment. I recalled the time my younger cousins Kevin, Jennifer, and I were body-blocked from seeing out Moozie's front door by our older teenage cousins, while they claimed to see Rudolph's nose leading Saint Nick's sleigh.

So, in honor and in memory of our Christmas celebrations past, the sisters gave birth to a new tradition, the "Christmas Adam Party," which was to take place the day before Christmas Eve, on December 23. Adam came before Eve, hence the name. Every relative was invited, and gifts were to be brought for all of the children under eighteen. Each family would continue our tradition by wrapping its gifts in a specific holiday paper and placing them together in a specified area for distribution later in the evening. Mom contacted "Uncle Wayne," no relation, a wonderful comic actor/musician and sort of a Shecky Green of a Santa, who agreed to lead the family in carols and draw caricatures of the children. Everyone sang carols, and the adults enjoyed Santa's risqué double entendres, which sailed over the innocent little ones' heads. Mom's home was alive with infectious excitement and joy, and the cacophonous laughter of all. It was a magical evening unlike any our family had experienced in years. We vowed to keep this new tradition alive.

As OFTEN HAPPENS, such great joy was followed by sorrow. Two days later Vilma passed, and one month later Mom's brother Uncle Donny did too, both from lung cancer. Three months later Mom was diagnosed with it as well. Tragedy following upon tragedy would decimate a weaker soul, but not Mother. She faced the grueling surgery with optimism, faith, and humor, as she had done so many times before. *Surrender* was a word foreign to her vocabulary; survival with grace was all she knew.

Mom underwent a lengthy operation to remove nearly an entire lobe of her lung. Cracked open like an egg, the incision tore across her chest, reaching halfway to her spine. Awaiting an encouraging report from the doctor, her family and a multitude of friends endured hours in the waiting room. His news was unsettling at best. The procedure had been more invasive than he had originally thought it would need to be, and given her age and other medical conditions, the next few hours would be quite difficult.

Dread came over me. *This might be it,* I thought. Her body and spirit had endured so much over the years, and maybe now it was time. A gentle nurse escorted Jay and me to the recovery room, warning us that Mother would be unable to speak due to the breathing tube. It might be there for days, she explained somberly. It wasn't a good sign. We prepared ourselves for the worst, anticipating the same kind of grim scene of pain and suffering that we witnessed on our way to recovery.

There she was. No makeup, no silk, no pearls—and no breathing tube. She smiled gently and wheezed, "Oh, my boys."

Worried, I asked the attending nurse where the tube was, and she grinned as she replied, "Miss Gayle can breathe on her own already; you boys got one tough mama."

She improved slowly, finally returning home after two weeks. On one of my many visits, I couldn't help noticing a strange addition to the numerous framed photos of family and friends decorating her lacy feminine bedroom, which I had decorated. Scattered about were a rather odd and unfamiliar array of medals bearing the relief images of saints, as well as vials of water, statuettes of saints, a loaf of bread, and a silver goblet. This was out of character and seemed a tad fundamentalist, so I asked, "Mom, what is all this stuff? Is this holy water?"

"Pumpkin, that is Lourdes water that Aunt Carol brought, and it's blessed and has healing powers, and that over there is the body and blood of Christ."

A soft but solid "Amen, sister" was heard from Miss Yvonne, Mother's Amazonian born-again and bejeweled sitter.

"Mother, who is this?" I asked, picking up a small medallion.

"That happens to be the blessed Father Silos. He watches over the sick. Miss Alma brought that medal, his picture, and everyone's favorite priest, Father Bouterie, did a blessing."

"Mother, we are not Catholic, we are Methodist, I think. Now that you are trying new religions, have you called the Dalai Lama or Rabbi Cohen?"

"If you must know, mister smarty pants, Mrs. Katz and her friends are saying prayers for me at Temple Sinai, and if I knew any Hindus, or Buddhists for that matter, I'd welcome their prayers or chants. You can say what you want, Bryanny boy, but I like it, it makes me feel better. You're the one that's always saying there are many roads—well, who knows? Father Silos needs only one more miracle to become a saint, and it could be with me. Just what New Orleans needs, a real saint."

Yvonne chimed in, "Amen, sister."

I have my issues with organized religion and cafeteria-style religion, picking and choosing certain dogmas that apply or seem ethical while ignoring the oppressive, non-inclusive, and outdated ones as if they don't exist. The trouble began a long time ago when we tried to bring God indoors. Leave it to mankind to screw it up and to Christians to turn heaven into an exclusive country club. But today was not the time to engage in a debate.

Just as with Moozie and Dad, the grim accoutrement of the invalid (what a horrible word, *in-valid*)—the hospital bed, walker, bed pan, oxygen tank, breathing apparatus—filled the room. These foreign contraptions no longer frightened me, but saddened me profoundly, because for the first time I saw my special friend, this darling enigma of a mother, seriously confronting her mortality. In her seventy-five years she had undergone over two dozen surgeries, and now her body was weak, depressed, and heartbroken. The worst part was that I saw sadness that was so foreign to her in her eyes—eyes that had always danced. We stared at each other briefly and intuitively.

I kissed her gently on the forehead so as not to cause any unnecessary pain. Though slightly more wheezy, she uttered in a lilt that could charm the husk right off an ear of corn, "Baby dear, Miss Margaret, Mr. Albert's sister, is coming to do my hair today—can you believe he broke his teasing hand? Thank the Lord, because I look like a wet rat."

My cousin Donna-Gayle, who now had become my mother's caretaker, secretary, bookkeeper, and confidante, gave a slight chuckle.

"Now, doodlebug, could you help me make it look presentable before she comes, just get my teasing comb off the vanity and try to fix it, please?"

I barely recall the last time I saw my mother's hair actually move. Since our emotional meeting at my birth many years ago, her 'do had consistently resembled a cotton-candy confection, strategically coiffed and lacquered. It has never been seen wet, or experienced the slightest hint of kinetic activity. Briefly in the late seventies there was a period when bejeweled or floral combs held back a few locks, but before the slightest breeze was allowed to disturb the creation, an ample coating of All Set was applied.

Every word my mother spoke took effort, and if she moved ever so slightly, she felt shocks of stabbing pain that brought tears to both our eyes. Having had some experience with character makeup and hair in various plays and musicals, I thought for a moment there was a chance, but it would definitely take a miracle of Father Silos to transform that mop of straw to its former glory. But try I would. During the teasing, spraying, and virtual molding of her tresses, we chatted about family, memories, and all that we'd been through. A gentle ease came over us with each brushstroke of blush, and as I was helping her put on her eyeliner, Mom looked up at me and whispered somberly, "Did I do this, pumpkin-eater boy? Did I help make you this way?"

"What way?"

"Sweet."

"Let's just say I had a wonderful teacher."

She smiled and started to well up, so I quickly joked, "I thought you meant gay. Oh, you can't take credit for that, it's all mine."

She started to smile, then to laugh, but the pain from her surgery stifled any outward expression of humor except in her eyes, those generous, knowing, always loving eyes.

"Oh pet, I think I may have to . . . Donna, Yvonne, I need some help to the loo, this is what we have been praying for!"

As Yvonne helped Mother to her failing feet, Donna, in a hushed voice, quickly and stealthily explained that she had not made "number two" in almost a week, and that per the suggestion of Yvonne, a potty vigil had become part of the daily ritual. Donna reassured Mom that she was on her way.

"Nan-Nan, just start without me." Then, aside to me, she muttered hopefully, "I hope this is it, 'cause I don't know the Hail Mary."

Not all that shocked, but seriously amused, I watched as the ladies fluttered through the beautiful yet eternally disheveled boudoir and into the adjoining loo, and shut the door. For some odd reason, which a therapist would have a field day deciphering, I remained.

Miss Yvonne's booming voice was the first to be heard.

"Y'all, let's all hold hands. Bow our heads. Dear Father God, we ask you to help Miss Gayle, we ask you to work through her, we know you work in mysterious ways."

There was the unmistakable sound of flatulence, followed by . . .

"Thank you, Jesus, amen."

"Come on, Miss Gayle, believe, let the spirit move you."

With that profound declaration came a thunderous "Hallelujah!"

The reverberating bellow nearly scared the crap out of me, so I can only imagine what effect it had on Mom. The result must have been an overwhelming success, because the next words were, "Praise Him, ask and ye shall receive, amen, amen, amen!"

Donna-Gayle burst from the room. Stifling her laughter, she grabbed my hand and forced me downstairs.

"Oh my God, Bryan, open some wine, I need a drink and a cigarette."

We both doubled over and, laughing hysterically, agreed that the phrase "holy shit" would have new meaning for us—forever and ever, amen.

Good News and Bad News

"Now, sweet potato, I don't want to slow you down, you have so much going on, but if it's okay, and you don't think I'd be a burden, I'd love to come out and see you do your thing in L.A., but I'll understand if . . . " Mom went on, muttering in her now slightly breathless style.

The removal of three-quarters of a lung a few years back, coupled with the effects of chemotherapy, was beginning to take its toll. Her signature honey-toned cotton-candy hair had fallen out and was replaced by a wiry gray Brillo pad. It didn't seem to faze her in the least; she wore hats and wigs, and continued to smile as she always had. She did everything in her power to fight this disease yet again, not just medically, but spiritually as well. Visualization classes, seminars on self-healing, meditation—if it might help her, she was going to try it.

"Mother, I would not have invited you if I didn't mean

it. Book your flight, use your miles to upgrade, and I'll make reservations at a hotel, one with no stairs."

"You are an angel. This may be my last opportunity to come out. Oh, baby dear, this is just what the doctor ordered, but if it's going to be too much for you . . ."

"Mom, you and Donna are coming—that's final."

Just then there came a knock on my trailer door. "You are invited on set." I've never understood why that phrase is used to call actors to the set. It's my job; I really don't need to be invited to work.

"Mom, I'll call you later, just get here, love you, 'bye."

Her choice of words—*last opportunity*—stuck in my head, and while making a last-minute tie adjustment, I realized that this was the first time she had ever slightly suggested the possibility of her death. Throughout her entire life, life itself was the answer, the simple driving force from which she never deviated. It was such a shock to me to hear that it sent my mind swimming.

As I crossed the scalding summer streets of the Los Angeles Center Studios and opened the double doors to the arctic air conditioning of the sound stage, I kept repeating the mantra I'd adopted very early in my career: "Leave your personal life at the stage door." I tried, but those two words plagued me. I had buried my father nearly twenty-five years before, and realized how lucky I was to have had my mother all these years, how wonderful and unique our friendship was. I thought of the years she'd fought just to stay alive, and how she'd survived countless life-threatening illnesses with dignity and grace, and was now waging a battle with her own destiny once again. When or how would it end? Where had it come from, this strength, this will?

As I passed a gathering of impeccably costumed 1960s secretaries, I smiled a hello and noticed that one actress was holding a pair of my mother's gloves, ones that I had given Janie, our brilliant costume designer, a year ago. I had come to terms with my mother's illness and the fact that the end could be soon. I had no regrets, and was fully prepared to release her; the problem was releasing myself. Tears started to well, and for a moment I thought I was about to lose it as I approached my friend Rich Sommer, who played *Mad Men*'s Harry Crane. He looked at me, and his face dropped.

"What's wrong? How's your mom?"

I took a deep breath to compose myself, then said, "She's coming to the premiere."

"That's fantastic! So why the who-died face?" he joked.

"It's just, it just really hit me that it's going to happen. I mean I have always known it will—hell, all of my youth and adult life I was constantly worrying about it. It's the natural progression, it's what should and must happen. It's the pain and suffering, *her* pain and suffering—it just sucks."

"I know what you mean; my grandmother died last year of cancer—no fun, there is no fun in a funeral. Hey, they're not ready for us just yet, the corn nuts are calling me at craft services, care to join?"

We laughed as we made our way past the huge lights and period sets. It still amazes me how such an unreal world can be transformed by the camera to appear so rich and real. Just like my own.

A WEEK LATER I was driving to LAX to retrieve Mom and Donna. Driving along La Cienega, I thought about my New York life and how everyone had thought that I would hate L.A., but maybe my time in New Orleans had tempered the culture shock. The one thing that L.A. has over the rest of the world is the perfect weather ninety-five percent of the year. It is mind-boggling how beautiful it is, but it explains why God saw fit to hurl the occasional mud slide, fire, or earthquake. En route to the airport, the sky was ablaze with the beginning of a perfect sunset, and the silhouettes of palm trees danced against skies of flame. Just minutes from the airport, my cell phone rang. It was Donna.

"Well, we are here, headed to baggage claim. Her majesty is now officially friends with everyone in the first-class cabin and many in coach, and she has made everyone in earshot promise they'll watch the season premiere of the show."

"I'll be there in a couple of minutes; just wait outside. And Donna, thank you for doing this."

As I approached the pickup area, I could see in the distance a wheelchair encircled by people, some standing, some actually kneeling, and as I got closer I saw that of course it was Mom, holding court with her new comrades as they were saying their good-byes.

I hugged Donna and made my way to my mother. When

I caught her brilliant twinkling gaze, my heart just smiled at the sight of her. There she was, seated in a wheelchair, dressed in a black pantsuit and pearls, and on her head was a matching black turban with a serious gold and pearl brooch centered on her forehead. She exclaimed, "Come give me a kiss, my angel boy. Y'all, this is my actor son Bryan, and he's on that television show I was singing the praises of, *Mad Men* on AMC Sunday nights at ten p.m., nine Central. That's when it airs where we live, in New Orleans. Oh, petunia, it's so good to see your sweet face, it just does my heart good."

I loaded the car as the other passengers went on their way, and as I approached Mom to help her into the car, she was handing the attendant who wheeled her a tip. "Thank you so much, Mercedes, I had an aunt Mercedes, Bryan, you remember Aunt Mercedes and Uncle Frank, that was my mother's brother and his wife, Bryan, this is Mercedes, and she has been a living doll, just a doll. You have been so sweet and you keep on taking those classes and one day you will be a great medical assistant, we need more sweet people like you."

With that, Mercedes hugged Mom and we went through the routine of her angling her bad hips and knees into my mini-SUV. The sunset was in full bloom, and the tall, spindly palms swayed in the gentle summer breeze now against a sky that glowed like lava.

"This is just beautiful, isn't it, Donna? Honey, tell me everything. How is filming? Are you excited about the premiere tomorrow, 'cause we are, I am about to bust, just bust with excitement!"

I started to answer, but Mom quickly said, "Now, honey, please take it easy, we are not in a race to get to the hotel and we would like to arrive in one piece, so please slow down. I don't want you to get a citation."

I pointed out that you can actually get a ticket for going too slow on the L.A. freeways, and that I knew what I was doing. I asked about everyone in the family, a subject she always loves to chat about.

"Well, Jay had the back surgery and was recovering just fine but the poor thing developed kidney stones again. I hear they are excruciating. You know your father had them something awful one year during Carnival. You and Jay were just little tykes at the time, and I was sitting in the box seat at one of the balls, to tell the truth I can't remember which one, was it Dorians or Osiris? . . . Well, anyhoo, I was waiting for him to dance with me for the first 'call out' dance, and no John, and the second dance, no John. Your Uncle Donny was his committeeman, so I asked him 'Where's Johnny?' and he had no idea, so he went backstage at the auditorium. As it turned out, your daddy had passed the kidney stone in the shower and fainted for a moment from the pain. Isn't that just horrible? So say a prayer for Jay-boy. Andrée is great, and the girls are getting more grown up every day, becoming little ladies. We went out to dinner the other night with Aunt Carol and Uncle Jack and had a fantastic time. Oh, pet, as we drive, please point out any sites of interest or historic significance. You know your grandfather Pa-paw, my father, wanted to move to California to retire, but Moozie could never leave New Orleans. Come to think of it, your daddy loved California too, but with the business and then his heart, he couldn't leave, and to tell the truth, me either. I just adore that city."

We drove up to the uber-chic London Hotel on San Vicente, and Mom marveled that there were no stairs and at the ultra-modern decor. Both she and Donna oohed and ahhed over the golden leather settee, commenting how different and festive it looked, but how it would never ever work in a real home. Once again she started to charm the doormen and valets and front-desk workers as she checked in.

Donna and I managed the luggage as well as the grocery order I had received. Prunes, bottled water, fresh fruit, and whole-wheat crackers. I added a bottle of Chardonnay for Donna and me, as Mom was not imbibing. She knew that when dealing with cancer, sweets are out and liquor just makes you sicker. I shared a glass with Donna, and we all stepped out onto the veranda for a quick toast to the twinkling lights of Hollywood. Mom slipped her braceleted arm around me and hugged tightly yet softly, saying, "Have I told you how proud I am of you?"

"Only all my life."

I informed them that I was filming tomorrow, and depending on the schedule, which could change at a moment's notice, the car would pick them up for the premiere first, then me. There were kisses, and I was on my way to my rented West Hollywood bungalow. I decided to bring my suit for the premiere to the studio just in case we ran late filming, which turned out to be the best decision, as we were extremely behind schedule that day. I called the press office and told them to have the driver pick Mom and Donna up from the hotel, then come downtown to get me. They arrived as I was wrapping, and our sweet assistant director and script supervisor took the girls on a tour of the Sterling Cooper set as I flew to my trailer and got dressed. Tying the vintage pink Pucci tie, one of my dad's that he had never worn, once again I caught a glimpse of him looking back at me in the mirror. He really wasn't the pink Pucci type, but I sure as hell am, and damn proud of it.

Rushing and trying so hard not to sweat, I made it to the car as Mom was returning from the "little ladies' room" on the arm of a charmed grip. Begging for as much air conditioning as the Lincoln Town car could blast, we were finally on our way to the screening and premiere party. For the premiere of season one, there were maybe four photographers as we entered the Friars' Club. For the second season premiere, there was a nice bank of press along the entrance of the Egyptian Theatre on Hollywood Boulevard. For this one, season three, the lobby of the Directors' Guild Theater was literally packed with photographers and press. At first I think Mom was overwhelmed and nearly blinded by all the flashes, but I leaned down and whispered, "Crazy, huh? Now watch me. You start looking left and slowly turn your head to the right."

All of the cast were so kind when meeting her, as were my dear friends who were able to attend, and she was on cloud nine throughout the entire experience. Of course she had to use the little girls' room yet again, and given her current physical condition, it takes her a bit longer than it does the average seventy-eight-year-old. Donna and she emerged just in time to be seated as speeches were made by AMC's president, Charlie Collier, and the show's creator, Matt Weiner. As the lights dimmed, I realized that I had completely forgotten to warn Mom about the carnal scene that was about to unfold involving my character, Salvatore Romano, and a provocative exchange with a willing bellhop in the season-three premiere episode. I took her hand and simply said, "Mom, there's a scene that gets a little sexy . . . with a bellhop . . . some kissing . . ."

"Pumpkin," she whispered, "I can't wait."

After the gasp-inducing lusty romp between Sal and his bellhop, culminating with many impassioned kisses and his hand down my pants, Mom looked at me, raised her eyebrow, then winked and giggled. The rest of the episode played beautifully, to overwhelming cheers from the audience. My heart was filled with pride, but more so with gratitude to Matt and the writers for entrusting me with such a big storyline, and in the season premiere, no less! But most of all for the fact that Mom was with me. She had been there for Rudolph the Red-Nosed Reindeer and seen every other performance since then, the good, the bad, and the ugly, and believe me there was a lot of ugly along the way. But after every show, after every performance, whether a huge Broadway hit or a tiny off-off-Broadway flop in a church basement, she was always smiles and praise, smiles and praise. As we exited the theater, friends and colleagues offered their congratulations upon meeting her, and she just graciously smiled and purred, "Now those are easy words for a mother's ears to hear."

In the car to the party, Mom was fluttering with excitement, but starting to fade. It had been a long day for her, and she said that she and Donna might have to make it an early night. A brief moment of quiet passed, then, breaking the short-lived silence, she asked, "Now, pet, tell me something. When Tom is out here with you, does he hear your lines and help you rehearse and all?"

I answered, "Yes, Mom, he does and he's really great and helps me a lot. Tom is a natural director and actor."

To which she quickly replied, "Well, I bet you two had some fun rehearsing that scene!"

She laughed hysterically at her little joke, so much that it became infectious and Donna and I joined in, laughing uncontrollably until we reached the party site, all of it lost on our driver, who must have thought us insane. And we were.

MOM AND DONNA returned to the balmy Deep South the next day, and Mom was able to have her next treatment of chemotherapy, which seemed to sit well with her this time, causing significantly fewer side effects than usual. She spoke on the phone with Tom at the shop, reliving all the moments of the premiere, thanking him for letting her go with me in his place. He would be with me in New York for the official premiere.

She gushed, "Sweetheart, you are just a dear, I am so

lucky to have you as a son-in-law; I just count my blessings every day that I was blessed with such wonderful
partners for my two boys. You and Andrée are just angels.
She is such a great mother and wife, and, well, you are just
perfect with Bryan."

She leaned back ever so slightly, and somehow lost her
balance, falling backward onto the cold tile floor of the
kitchen. Tom later told me he had never heard screams of
pain so anguishing. The telephone receiver had fallen, and
he could hear her call for help, mixed with animal cries of
agony. He heard Donna come rushing in to call 911, hung
up the phone, and ran out of the shop. He actually arrived
at her home before the paramedics.

Jay called me in L.A. with the news that Mom might
have broken her hip, and as it turned out, that was exactly
what happened. She'd shattered her femur in three places
and needed serious surgery, including a rod and screws. *This
is it,* I thought, speaking with my godchild Ramsey, who
was now the charge nurse on the orthopedic recovery floor
of East Jefferson Hospital. She informed me that this was
not good, not good at all. *What next?* I thought. How much
more could she take? People her age, in her condition, rarely
recovered from such a break. The doctors had to wait a few
days to make sure her Coumadin levels were right, as she
was subject to life-threatening blood clots, but when all was
set, she sailed through the surgery with no complications.

I now had completely given in to the fact that it was
just a matter of time. I cried for a few minutes as I had
when I'd learned of my father's death, but then it was time

to get to work, to get home. As soon as possible, I flew into Louis Armstrong Airport and made my way to the hospital. Preparing for the worst, I realized my true job, my sole purpose, was to try to take her mind off the pain and, as always, entertain. That I could do, and that I would. As I exited the elevator at the ninth floor, Ramsey and I locked eyes, and she could see the heartbreak in my face.

She smiled as she hugged me, saying in a calming tone, "B, she is really doing well. We are amazed. Go in and see her; you're not going to believe it."

I knocked and opened the door, and there she was—lipstick on, a bit of blush, and a turban to match her bed coat. My mother's eyes lit up as I entered. "Oh, baby dear, you are a sight for sore eyes and a sore hip." We hugged, and she introduced me to her sitter, Mary, who was preparing her lunch tray. "Mary, this is my son Bryan, he's on the show *Mad Men* I told you about, on AMC Sundays at ten p.m., nine Central. Mary is just the sweetest. Oh, what do we have today—is it Galatoire's or Commander's Palace?" she joked about the dreary hospital food. "Oh, and Mary's a deacon at her church, so we have wonderful prayers, isn't that just perfection, pet?"

"Nice to meet you, Mary; she must have you jumping already."

Mary laughed softly. "Oh, we are just having a grand time, ain't that right, Miss Gayle?"

"Most definitely," Mom said. "Doodle bug, I'm not supposed to have sweets, because I really need to lose more weight, both of my doctors agree that it will help me with the healing. I know how much you love bread pudding, so join me for this delicious luncheon, I've already got my hat on, pecan."

A LITTLE OVER six weeks later, Tom and I were actually taking her to dinner at Commander's Palace, where for generations our family had shared so many celebratory dinners and jazz brunches. Family friends had been the proprietors, and now the Grand Dame of New Orleans cuisine was in the able hands of the next generation of Brennan descendants. Mom was dressed in a smashing red ensemble complete with a matching red turban, and the crowning detail, the two bee pins, talking to each other. As she entered the Palace, she was received as if she were Dolly Levi entering the Harmonia Gardens. She walked steadily with her walker in hand until she reached the best table in the house, the corner banquette.

As the fluster caused by her arrival calmed, and after we sat, and were slightly settled, Mom said gently, "My dears, I have a little announcement to make. Today, as you may know, the results came in of all my tests, and I have some good news and some bad news. The good news is that my hip is healing beautifully and I'll be back on my cane within a month. The cancer has still not metastasized anywhere in my entire body. The brain scan came back negative—no jokes just yet, please; the doctors were worried about the aneurysm. And three of the six tiny tumors in my chest area are undetectable and the other three have grown insignificantly! Isn't that just splendid news?!"

We burst into cheers, tears, and applause, and finally I asked what the bad news was.

"Well, I'm doing so well that if I continue this way, the doctor will be able to do my knee replacement in a few months. Well, I guess that isn't such bad news when everything is said and done. Now, I don't know about you good people, but I am going to celebrate with just one cocktail." With that, our favorite waiter approached.

"I overheard some happiness at this table, Mrs. Batt. Are we celebrating something special, I hope?"

"As a matter of fact, we are, darling," Mom lilted. "It's sort of my birthday in a way."

He replied, smiling, "Oh, Mrs. Batt, we've been hoping. What can I bring you?"

She smiled as she placed her perfectly manicured finger to her cheek in girlish thought, and one hand on his. "Now, sweetheart, this will eventually be a martini, but I would just adore a Ketel One, up icy, icy cold so that those bitsy shards of ice are just floating on the top, a teensy bit dirty, with a twist, and almond-stuffed olives on the side."

I glanced across at my sweet mother, her eyes dancing with hope, hope she has always possessed, hope she has never lost faith in, and hope she has always given to me and everyone she has touched in her beautiful life. I thought for a moment of how this story would and must end one day, but for this night and right now and forever, I would celebrate this magical and ineffable great lady. She ain't heavy, she's my mother.

ACKNOWLEDGMENTS

I am so grateful to everyone who made this book possible, my dear friends, mentors, and family, especially Gayle, John, Jay, Andree, Bailey, and Kelly Batt. Thanks also to my literary agent, Eric Myers, and editor, Julia Pastore, as well as the diligent and enthusiastic team at Harmony Books. If it were not for the unswerving support and encouragement of Katy Danos, this book would have never happened. And most of all, a heartfelt thank-you to Tom Cianfichi, who gave me a laptop a few Christmases ago with a card simply saying "write your stories."

ABOUT THE AUTHOR

Bryan Batt (actor, designer, civic activist) portrays Salvatore Romano in AMC's critically acclaimed drama *Mad Men*. The hit TV series has been presented with a multitude of awards and honors, including Emmys, Golden Globes, and the Screen Actors Guild and Peabody Awards.

As a Broadway veteran, his leading and principal roles include: 2005 revival of *La Cage aux Folles, Beauty and the Beast, Suessical the Musical, Sunset Boulevard, Saturday Night Fever, The Scarlet Pimpernel, Joseph and the Amazing Technicolor Dreamcoat, Starlight Express,* and *Cats*. Off Broadway he has appeared in *Forbidden Broadway* (Drama Desk Nomination). Theatrically, Bryan is most proud of originating the role of Darius in both the New York and Los Angeles (Drama-Logue Award) productions as well as the film adaptation of Paul Rudnick's groundbreaking comedy *Jeffrey*.

Bryan and his partner of twenty years, Tom Cianfichi, are the nationally recognized creative forces behind Hazelnut (www.hazelnutneworleans.com), a fine gift and home accessories shop in Bryan's hometown of New Orleans. Hazelnut has been featured in the *New York Times, House Beautiful, InStyle, Traditional Home, Southern Accents,* and more.

Bryan, a civic activist, champions many causes, including Broadway Cares/Equity Fights AIDS, Habitat for Humanity, Second Harvest Food Bank, the Human Rights Campaign (Equality Award), the ASPCA, the Preservation Resource Center, the Point Foundation, New Orleans AIDS Task Force, and Le Petit Theatre du Vieux Carré.

Bryan lives tri-coastally with Tom and their Boston terrier, Peggy, splitting time among New Orleans, New York, and Los Angeles.

www.BryanBatt.com